Cooking Without

Cooking Without

RECIPES FREE FROM ADDED GLUTEN, SUGAR, DAIRY PRODUCTS, YEAST, SALT AND SATURATED FAT

Barbara Cousins

HarperCollins*Publishers*

Thorsons
An Imprint of HarperCollins*Publishers*
77–85 Fulham Palace Road
Hammersmith, London W6 8JB
1160 Battery Street,
San Francisco, California 94111–1213

First published by Barbara Cousins 1989
Published by Thorsons 1997

10 9 8 7 6 5

© Barbara Cousins 1997

Barbara Cousins asserts the moral right to
be identified as the author of this work

A catalogue record for this book is available
from the British Library

ISBN 0 7225 3457 4

Printed and bound in Great Britain
by Caledonian International Book Manufacturing Ltd, Glasgow

Contents

Foreword

Improving your health through diet can be daunting unless you have some help with creating appetizing menus. We all know what we shouldn't eat, but what do we do with those healthy ingredients like brown rice, vegetables and pulses? Few cookery books dwell on them for long, and those that do usually combine them with flour, butter or margarine, cheese, eggs and other dairy products. That's not much help for someone who is serious about trying to work on a long-standing health problem, or even if you are just trying to discover whether you have any food allergies.

Barbara Cousins is a working nutritional therapist, and her book has arisen out of the need to help many people find ways to really enjoy food cooked without all those ingredients we so often take for granted. I have not come across any other book which contains so many recipes using vegetables in appetizing ways. Now that the World Health Organization is advising all of us to eat at least five portions of fruit and vegetables every day, good recipes are vitally important, and you are sure to find some in *Cooking Without* that you will treasure and use over and over again.

Linda Lazarides

Introduction

This book is about health – how to gain it and how to keep it. Be aware that health is not a mere absence of disease but a positive feeling of wellbeing which embraces mental, emotional and spiritual as well as physical health. This book is about the nutritional aspects of health, the dos and don'ts of healthy eating because, quite simply, 'we are what we eat'. By giving the body a sufficient amount of the nutrients it needs, it has the best opportunity to heal itself and to stay well.

Detoxification

The two main causes of health problems are toxicity and malnutrition. In Western society, we are generally overfed but undernourished. If our bodies receive sufficient good quality fuel (such as vitamins and minerals) then they will be aided to work more efficiently and to overcome any toxicity (substances which should not be present in the body). Similarly, if we receive insufficient amounts of essential nutrients our toxic load may be allowed to rise to levels which promote illness.

WHERE DOES TOXICITY COME FROM?

In my opinion, the main sources of toxicity are as follows:

- Some toxicity in food is natural, such as solanine in potatoes. Most, however, is unnatural, such as fungicides, pesticides, colourings, flavourings and stabilizers.
- Industrial emissions, cigarette smoke and exhaust fumes pollute our atmosphere.
- Our drinking water is polluted by both industry and farming as well as by chemicals used to 'cleanse' it.
- Most drugs contain toxins, including over-the-counter reme-

dies such as laxatives, painkillers and indigestion tablets. Alcohol is also a poison.
- Around our homes, deodorants, perfumes, washing-up liquid and other cleaning fluids are chemically derived toxic substances which are absorbed to a certain extent by our bodies.
- Bottled-up feelings and emotions constitute emotional toxicity which in turn affects our physical body.

Toxicity and Health

It is impossible for us to avoid toxins completely. Indeed, our bodies are built to cope with a certain amount, the liver being our main organ of detoxification. Toxins are naturally removed from our bodies through urine and faeces, sweating and expiration (breathing out). It is only when eliminating channels cannot cope with this removal that the body will let us know that all is not well (illness).

Often symptoms of illness are the body using its overflow system to remove excess toxicity. The safest place for excess toxins to overflow is through the skin, as this is farthest away from the vital organs and enables toxicity to be removed to the outside world. The boils and carbuncles so common in the past were the result of elimination through the skin. Nowadays, these are less common. Even those teenagers who live on chocolate and chips frequently have good complexions. It takes a certain amount of vitality for the body to eliminate through the skin, and at present many individuals do not have constitutions strong enough for this process. Eliminating through the skin causes health problems such as psoriasis, eczema, rashes, itching, dandruff, boils and spots.

Even if the body does not have the vitality to use the skin successfully to eliminate excess toxins, it does not give up trying. The next safest place for it to use is the internal mucosa, that is any moist orifices open to the outside world. Eliminating through the mucosa causes illnesses such as coughs, colds, catarrh, diarrhoea, colitis, thrush, cystitis, conjunctivitis, ulcers and heavy, clotted periods.

Individuals who still have excess toxicity, even though they may be using some of the above methods to eliminate them, will suffer from symptoms related to toxicity being deposited in the body, usually in the areas of least resistance. These areas vary from person to person, and are dependent on factors such as hereditary conditions, illnesses and injuries. Tiredness, irritability, anxiety, depression, arthritis, high blood pressure, heart problems and cancer can all be promoted by toxicity.

Needless to say, everyone can benefit from a period of detoxification, whether they have serious health problems, just feel below par or are healthy and want to make sure they stay that way.

The Health Benefits of Cooking Without

Following the eating regime outlined in this book will reduce the toxic load and improve the level of nutrients available to the body. Also, because the diet is easy for the body to assimilate, the food travels quickly through the digestive tract. This not only assists the removal of toxins, but because the body's workload is reduced, also releases extra energy for healing and elimination. Additionally, the diet is designed to support the body's blood sugar, and by doing so, not only does the individual feel better but every organ and system in the body feels healthier and works more efficiently too.

Blood Sugar

We need sugar in order to fuel our bodies and our brains, but it needs to be in the right form. The sugar we find in biscuits and sweets and add to our tea is not a good fuel. This sugar has been overprocessed and is too readily absorbed by the body. It causes a sudden surge of sugar to enter the bloodstream. Because too much sugar in the bloodstream is harmful, the pancreas must produce extra insulin to remove this excess. In order to do this, the pancreas needs fuel and energy, and so eating sugar robs our body of vital nutrients and overworks the pancreas.

If, however, we eat sugar in the form of complex carbohydrate foods (such as rice, millet and root vegetables) then the body slowly breaks it down into simple sugars (glucose) which are steadily released into the bloodstream to give us sustained energy. If we eat more at a particular meal than the body needs, then the excess glucose is converted into glycogen and stored by the liver so that, mid-morning or mid-afternoon, we can have a top-up of blood sugar.

Unfortunately, not everyone's liver releases blood sugar efficiently. This is usually because the liver is struggling to cope with excess toxins and a lack of nutrients. As far as the body is concerned, removal of excess toxins is more important than giving the body or brain energy, and there is a tendency for the liver to say, 'Sit down if you are tired or cannot think straight – I've got too much to do'! Hence, many individuals develop cravings for sugary snacks in order to boost their blood sugar, and the vicious circle starts again. Tea, coffee and cigarettes are also used to boost blood sugar – they do this by kicking the adrenal glands into action (see below).

An alternative way to produce energy is by living on adrenalin, which causes blood sugar to be released. Adrenalin is designed for emergency situations – the 'flight or fight' response – and is not meant to be experienced daily. Nowadays, many individuals have adrenal glands which are becoming exhausted due to overuse. At one end of the scale are individuals who feel tired and always seem to be pushing themselves to keep going, and at the other end we have those suffering from illnesses such as ME (myalgic encephalomyelitis), *see page 18*. In between are a list of symptoms related to low blood sugar (hypoglycaemia), and these can affect not only the physical body but also the mental and emotional states. They include fatigue, headaches, palpitations, weak or dizzy spells, cold sweats, cravings, unjustified fears, lack of concentration or a muzzy head, mental confusion, depression, anxiety, phobias, restlessness, moodiness, insomnia, night terrors, uncoordination and a lack of or excessive hunger. Low blood sugar also has an undermining effect on every other health problem.

By putting *Cooking Without* into practice, foods eaten at regular intervals are used to keep the blood sugar stable, thereby allowing the liver and adrenal glands to recover and the body to obtain sufficient energy to remove excess toxins. When the blood sugar is more stable you will be aware that your mood and your energy are more even and that you do not develop cravings. Other symptoms related to low blood sugar will also disappear.

When trying to improve health it is important to be aware that our bodies can only produce a certain amount of energy each day, and that this energy is needed for detoxification and healing. For instance, if you feel a little better and decide to catch up on all those jobs you have left undone, then you may start to feel poorly again because the energy has started going into the jobs rather than into healing. It is therefore important to allow a period of convalescence, when you try to conserve as much energy as possible for the body to use. Stress and worry can cause blood sugar to drop even though food may have been eaten at regular intervals, thus depleting the body's energy. In order to help your body heal itself, practise the art of relaxation and avoid stressful situations whenever possible.

One last point about blood sugar. Many individuals feel that their bodies need something sweet. They say that they have a 'sweet tooth', or feel that a meal is not a meal without a pudding. As far as I am concerned, there are two main reasons why we crave sweet things. One is because the blood sugar is low (this should not be the case once *Cooking Without* is put into practice); the second is because sweet foods are often used as a love substitute. This means that we work hard and push our bodies or give ourselves a hard time mentally by thinking about what we should be doing rather than treating ourselves with respect and kindness. Having punished ourselves, we suddenly crave something sweet in order to give back to ourselves. The fact that this sweet food often makes us feel worse, either because our blood sugar dips or because we feel guilty, causes a vicious circle to be set up. If you continue to crave sweet foods after putting this diet into practice, there may be an emotional problem which needs to be addressed (*see 'Emotions, addictions and ill health', page 20*).

Common Foods and Health Problems

WHEAT

Wheat as a dietary constituent has some advantages, but on the whole these are outweighed by its disadvantages. Wheat is generally thought of as a wholesome, nutritious, fibre-rich food, but unfortunately for many individuals (including many who do not realize), wheat is actually causing them problems.

Wheat contains gluten which, when wet, is a sticky glue-like substance. Not long ago, flour and water were used as a cheap glue. In our gut this glue can play havoc with the digestion and absorption of nutrients. Because gluten is so sticky and difficult to digest, it encourages the growth of unfriendly bacteria *(see 'Candida', page 13)* which are responsible for producing toxic substances and gas. Constipation, diarrhoea, bloatedness, indigestion, flatulence and wind are all problems that benefit from the removal of wheat from the diet.

Wheat is one of the most common foods that people become allergic to. It can make an individual feel tired, irritable and depressed, as well as aggravating other diseases, such as arthritis, psoriasis and eczema. Because most people eat wheat so often, the body adapts and copes, and they are unaware that it does not agree with them *(see 'Allergies', page 17)*. Once it is removed from the diet, however, many individuals notice tremendous improvements in their health and well-being.

Wheat has a suppressive action on the liver, so even individuals who seem to tolerate wheat well actually slow down their rate of elimination by eating wheat too often. Wheat is therefore best avoided in the early stages of elimination, especially if your health is seriously below par. After working on the eating regime outlined in this book to a point where you feel fit and healthy, try including wheat again, but never include it in large quantities and never more than once per day. Other grains that contain gluten are rye, oats and barley, and although some individuals may tolerate these better than wheat, others may need to avoid them completely until their health has improved.

MILK

Milk has an image of being the perfect food but it is perfect only when fed from the mother to her infant. A young child eventually loses the enzyme necessary to digest milk, and after this stage, milk becomes acid and mucous-forming, capable of upsetting normal bowel flora and preventing the absorption of vitamins and minerals. Many individuals develop allergies to milk and its products, and they are often unaware of this until milk is removed from the diet.

In general, we are led to believe that we do not obtain sufficient calcium and that milk and milk products are essential. However, calcium is readily available in foods such as vegetables, fruit, nuts and pulses. If there is a problem with inadequate calcium, it is far more likely to be through poor absorption than through poor intake, and it is more often the individuals who are intolerant of dairy produce who have the lowest calcium levels.

If you are unsure about your calcium levels it is best to have an osteoporosis check by your doctor and then to consult a qualified nutritional therapist for advice on supplementation, particularly if you have an intolerance to dairy produce.

If our diet and absorption are improved we can often live more healthily without milk. This can be seen in many tribal communities where milk and milk products are not consumed yet children grow well, producing good bones and teeth, and diseases such as arthritis and osteoporosis are unknown.

CHEESE

Cheese not only has the negative aspects of milk but it is also high in fat and salt and difficult to digest. Cottage cheese is more acceptable once health has been attained.

BUTTER

Butter is the fatty part of the milk, but because little of the milk remains, it can often be tolerated by those who cannot tolerate milk. If a form of fat is used for spreading, I think that butter is preferable to chemically derived margarines, but it should be used in moderation.

YOGURT

Live yogurt is the most favourable of all milk products due to the fact that it is low in fat and is partly digested by the action of the micro-organisms it contains. These micro-organisms assist in the repopulation of the intestinal tract with friendly bacteria. Yogurt does, however, still carry the negative aspects of milk and is often better tolerated if made from sheep or goat's milk.

FATS AND OILS

Fats and oils can be categorized into saturates, monounsaturates and polyunsaturates.

Saturated Fats
These are the ones we are constantly being told to cut down on, and all the recipes in this book are free from added saturated fat. I feel, however, that the reason our bodies do not cope well nowadays with saturated fat is because we are so full of toxins and lacking in vitamins and minerals. The liver, which is our main organ of detoxification, is also the principal organ that deals with fat. If the liver is struggling to detoxify, it will also be struggling to cope with fat.

The liver is also the organ that balances the production of cholesterol in the body. Cholesterol is a fat which has gained a bad reputation as far as health is concerned, its excess being associated with conditions such as heart attacks and strokes. But cholesterol is needed by the body for many different functions, and if we do not absorb sufficient amounts from our food, the liver is capable of making more. Equally, if we have too much cholesterol, the liver is capable of removing any excess by excreting it in the form of bile acids. In order to perform this cholesterol balancing act efficiently, however, the liver is dependent on an adequate supply of nutrients and energy being obtained from the diet. *Cooking Without* aims to supply these.

It is therefore important that we encourage a good bile flow. In order to do this we do need some fat in the diet as bile is released in response to fat or oil being digested. Therefore, do not completely remove fat or oil from your diet.

As well as excess cholesterol, toxicity is released from the liver via bile, and in order for both of these to be excreted from the body once they are in the digestive tract, adequate amounts of fibre are needed to assist their elimination. This prevents them from being reabsorbed into the body.

The diet outlined in this book enables an adequate intake of fat and plenty of fibre to be consumed. As far as I am concerned, the reason why our ancestors could eat a high-fat diet and not suffer from the rate of heart disease that afflicts modern society is that they had the necessary vitamins, minerals and fibre in their diets, and they were not overloaded with toxins.

It is best to limit saturated fats while detoxifying, but do not be obsessive about removing every scrap. Individuals are often told not to eat eggs because they are high in fat and cholesterol, but eggs also contain lecithin, a fat emulsifier, and are quite acceptable used in sensible quantities. Even lean meat contains saturated fat, and so it is sensible to eat a varied diet which contains some fish and a number of vegetarian days. Although coconut is of vegetable origin, its oil is the highest in saturated fat of all vegetable oils, and so it should be used sparingly. Butter, I feel, is the most acceptable substance for spreading and is quite admissible if used in small quantities.

Monounsaturated Fats
These include olive oil, and although little has been spoken of monounsaturates in the past, they are now being regarded as helpful fats in the diet (the Mediterranean diet contains plenty of olive oil). Olive oil is also the most stable oil when heated. All oils, however, become increasingly toxic when heated, so limit very hot frying. Do include some monounsaturated oil in your diet. You could add olives to suitable recipes or eat them as a snack, or

you could use olive oil in salad dressings or poured over rice or vegetables.

Polyunsaturated Oils

We have been constantly encouraged to use these oils, but this is not necessarily a good idea. All oils contain essential fatty acids but linolenic acid is the essential fatty acid of which we are most in need. This is obtained best from eating fish (preferably oily), green leafy vegetables or from linseed oil and linseeds.

Unfortunately, if we eat too many polyunsaturates, linolenic acid is outweighed by the linoleic acid found in polyunsaturated oils, and this causes an imbalance in our bodies. Therefore, polyunsaturated oils are best used in moderation with fish, green vegetables and linseed oil being consumed to provide a balance. Most margarines are made from polyunsaturates but they are also produced using chemicals and are then partly hydrogenated, which turns some of the polyunsaturates into saturated fat. The hydrogenation process also causes the production of free radicals (harmful substances) and changes the structure of the oil from a 'cis' form to a 'trans' form. This 'trans' form is rarely found in nature and is therefore unacceptable to the human body. Avoid the use of margarine unless you cannot tolerate butter, in which case find one of the margarines which is not hydrogenated and is labelled high in 'cis' form fatty acids.

Certain measures can be taken to safeguard the use of fats and oils in the diet:
1 Consume most oils in the form of foods, e.g. nuts, seeds, olives, beans, sweetcorn and linseeds.
2 Include some linseed oil in your daily diet to balance linoleic acid with linolenic acid. Linseeds can be bought from health-food shops and are pleasant to take, sprinkled on breakfast cereals, salads or in soups. Try taking 1–2 dsp per day for a real health benefit. Linseed oil can be taken from the spoon or used in salad dressings.
3 Use cold-pressed oils as heavily processed oils will have suffered oxidative and chemical damage.

4   Buy oils in small glass bottles and store in the fridge.
5   Improving nutrition will enable fats in any form to be more readily assimilated by the body.

SALT

Sodium is an essential mineral in the body, and together with potassium, magnesium and calcium, it forms one of the four bulk minerals. An over-consumption of salt upsets the delicate balance between these minerals, and the accumulation of sodium in the cells causes the latter to become more acidic. Other micro-minerals such as zinc and selenium, which the body may be deficient in, will not be readily absorbed unless the four bulk minerals are well balanced.

Our bodies do need some salt as sodium is lost through the skin and faeces. Approximately half a gram per day is needed, and this small amount can easily be obtained by eating natural foods such as vegetables.

Salt is not the only form of sodium to enter our bodies. Other forms include monosodium glutamate (used as a flavour enhancer), sodium bicarbonate (used in baking powder), sodium nitrate and nitrite (used as preservatives), and hydrolysed proteins (used in stock cubes).

Avoid adding salt to your food for at least three to four months. You will then start to taste the food rather than the salt, and you will find that many of the previous things you ate are now too salty. If salt is then needed in the occasional soup or casserole you will be able to add it in order to improve the taste. You should not need to put salt in cooked vegetables or grains or on the table.

Seaweed, although salty, is full of minerals and I feel it is acceptable in the small quantities that would be consumed.

SUGAR

If we ate sugar in its natural form of fruit or sugar cane, there would be a limit to how much sugar we could consume. Along with the sugar, we would obtain lots of fibre and the vitamins and minerals needed to digest the sugar. The fibre content means that it would take time to break down the structure and release the sugar into the bloodstream.

If, however, we eat manufactured sugar or products made from this (such as biscuits, cakes and sweets), we encourage low blood sugar or hypoglycaemia. This sudden surge of sugar into the bloodstream and its removal by the pancreas results in the roller coaster effects of cravings, highs and then lows which leave us feeling physically, mentally and emotionally below par *(see 'Blood Sugar', page 3)*. Sugar encourages the overgrowth of bad intestinal flora and should be avoided in all its forms. Brown sugar, although retaining some nutrients, still contains 97 per cent white sugar.

When health has been attained, a little honey, molasses or no-sugar fruit spread is acceptable.

YEAST AND FERMENTED PRODUCTS

Because yeast-related products can aggravate *Candida* symptoms and upset the digestive tract, it is best to avoid these products on a temporary basis and then watch how your body reacts as you reintroduce them at a later date. They include yeast, yeast extract, vinegar, citric acid, monosodium glutamate, stock cubes, tofu, miso, shoyu/tamari sauce, alcohol, cheese, mushrooms and dried fruit.

I find that mushrooms and tofu, if used in small quantities, are quite acceptable for many *Candida* sufferers. Dried fruit can also be used sparingly for many *Candida* sufferers, provided it is washed well to remove the yeasts on the surface. Some individuals, however, will have an intolerance or allergy to yeast and will need to remove all yeast and fermented products for a much longer period. This will enable the immune system to recover *(see 'Allergies and Intolerances', page 17)*. Miso, tamari and shoyu sauce are the most acceptable flavourings to use in cooking once health has been obtained, but individuals will need to test these to see how they react.

TEA AND COFFEE

Most people use tea and coffee to give them a lift. They do this because these beverages contain drug-like substances which kick the body and cause a release of blood sugar. This means that one is not working on natural energy but is flogging an otherwise 'dead horse'.

Try alternatives but be aware that it may take time for you to acquire a taste for them. Also accept that you will miss tea and coffee – remember they are drugs. Persevere and make the change-over gradually.

ADDITIVES

These include colourings, flavourings, preservatives, antioxidants, emulsifiers, stabilizers, sweeteners and modified starches.

Additives are mostly chemically derived and as such are another toxic substance for the body to deal with. Additives such as flavourings will often contain 100 different chemicals just to produce one flavour. They have been shown to cause epileptic fits, asthma and hyperactivity, but often the underlying damage is unseen. Learn to read labels before you buy, but do be aware that some additives are naturally derived and are acceptable.

Some Common Health Problems

CANDIDA ALBICANS

Inside our intestinal tract are minute organisms called intestinal flora. These are bacteria responsible in part for the absorption of nutrients and the elimination of waste products. Among these bacteria both good and bad exist, but normally the bad bacteria do not cause us any problems provided we have sufficient natural defences, or good bacteria, to keep them in their place. Nowadays, one particular bad bacteria, called *Candida*, is being encouraged to get out of hand, and its overgrowth is causing the individuals concerned a lot of problems. This overgrowth is being caused by the way we eat, chlorine in our water supplies and the widespread use of the pill, antibiotics and hormones (either taken as medication or consumed in meat).

Once out of hand, the *Candida* eventually punctures the gut wall. The wall, which is normally very particular about what it allows through, is now open to absorb larger particles, such as food which has not been completely digested, toxins from the gut and *Candida* itself. The immune system recognizes these particles as foreign, and should produce antibodies to protect us against further invasion. If, however, the immune system is overburdened with toxins and lacking in essential nutrients, then it is weakened and is unable to defend itself. *Candida* is allowed to spread unhampered into the body, and an immune response or allergy is set up. Both allergies and low blood sugar are frequent forerunners of *Candida*.

Here is a list of some of the symptoms which can be attributed to *Candida's* overgrowth. You will notice that some of the symptoms also fit into the list of hypoglycaemia symptoms *(see page 4)*:

- cystitis
- thrush
- fungal infections
- PMT
- endometriosis
- abdominal bloating
- indigestion
- flatulence
- diarrhoea
- constipation
- bad breath
- acne
- numbness
- tingling
- recurrent sore throats
- blurred vision
- lethargy

- mood swings
- anxiety
- depression
- muscle aches
- itching
- headaches
- muzziness
- dizziness
- lack of concentration
- memory lapses.

As can be seen from the above list, *Candida albicans* merits attention, but all too frequently the attention is directed obsessively at killing the *Candida* without reference to the individual's body which has allowed the invasion to take place. *Candida* is present in all of us and can never be completely eliminated. Therefore, working in isolation on trying to kill or starve the *Candida* means that, as soon as treatment stops, it will thrive again.

Candida grows in an acidic environment within the intestinal tract. The environment in the cells of a healthy body whose mineral status is good is slightly alkaline. Therefore, even if Candida reached these cells, in a healthy person its growth would be discouraged and it would die. However, what is happening nowadays is that our cells are becoming more acidic and our bodies and immune systems are unable to protect themselves against *Candida* invasion. Increased levels of acidity in the cells are being caused by the widespread consumption of acid-forming foods (such as meat, tea, coffee and alcohol) and a lack of alkaline-forming foods (mainly fruit and vegetables), together with the fact that a lot of the food we do eat is lacking in minerals, over-processed and laden with chemical additives.

The only real answer to *Candida* problems is to detoxify the body and replenish its mineral reserves. By working on the dietary regime outlined in this book, the cells will gradually lose their acidity and become slightly alkaline, the immune system will be strengthened and the *Candida* will no longer be able to take over.

Too many *Candida* diets cause individuals to starve themselves by excessively limiting foods. For instance, many *Candida* regimes remove carbohydrates completely. This is based on the theory that carbohydrates convert to sugar and sugar feeds *Candida*. However, limiting carbohydrates encourages toxic symptoms as toxins are released from the cells in response to fasting (hardly eating) or a diet which is high in vegetables and low in carbohydrates.

In order for this toxicity to be removed, the body needs energy (blood sugar) to work the elimination system. It also needs a medium which will soak up the acid waste or toxicity and remove it from the body. Complex carbohydrates are the only foods which fulfil these two roles. What is frequently termed 'die-off' in many *Candida* books and is supposedly caused by *Candida* dying and releasing its toxicity is, as far as I am concerned, a build up of toxins caused by eating insufficient quantities of the right kinds of foods. It happens with all patients who limit the quantity of food they eat, especially carbohydrates, whether they suffer from *Candida* symptoms or other problems.

The regime outlined in this book is ideal for *Candida* sufferers, even though it is high in carbohydrates. These carbohydrates are complex in form and will be tolerated by all except a very small minority who have allergies to certain foods. Care may be needed with fresh fruit, and dried fruit should be avoided initially and washed well to remove yeasts when introduced. Yeast and fermented products as well as cereals containing gluten are best avoided, and mushrooms may need to be avoided in the early stages.

On an emotional level, *Candida* sufferers are lacking in self-worth and are very hard on themselves *(see 'Emotions, Addictions and Ill Health', page 20)*. Even if they do not try to be Superman or Superwoman, they still push and expect too much of their bodies. The reasons that cause *Candida* sufferers to be so hard on themselves will be uncovered as detoxification takes place. These reasons, which can be termed emotional toxicity, will be eliminated along with the physical toxins present in the body.

ALLERGIES AND INTOLERANCES

Allergies and intolerances are very common nowadays, and many individuals spend a lot of time and money being tested to find the substances which are causing them problems. Merely avoiding these substances is not, however, the permanent answer to allergies. It is important to realize that unless one finds the root of the allergy problem (that is, why the individual has become allergic in the first place) the body will persist in producing more allergies, and its health will continue to deteriorate.

The immune system is a complex army of cells and antibodies which protect the body from external invaders. When working harmoniously, the immune system protects us from many microorganisms, some of which cause infectious diseases. However, when the cells of the body and immune system are overburdened with toxins, there is a tendency for the immune system to over-react to invaders. This causes the production of allergy symptoms. It can also cause a drop in blood sugar levels because of the stress the allergy creates. Mineral and vitamin deficiencies go hand in hand with excess toxicity and so aggravate the problem. *Candida* is often responsible for the immune system being invaded. As well as *Candida*, partly digested food and toxins from the gut reach the immune system once the gut wall has been punctured.

Many individuals are affected by allergies which can be termed 'hidden' or 'masked' allergies. This means that they do not produce symptoms which are typically linked to allergies, such as spots or rashes, but these masked allergies are undermining health in a more subtle way. The foods or substances which cause masked allergies tend to be the ones we come into contact with on a fairly regular basis, such as bread or milk. In these cases, individuals can get hooked on the food causing problems and so crave and temporarily feel better for eating this food. Once it is removed from the diet, however, many individuals notice tremendous improvements in their health and state of well-being.

It is obviously useful in the short term to remove the main foods likely to cause allergy problems, but in order to obtain long-term benefits, toxins must be removed from the cells of the immune system, and the vitamin and mineral depletion in the cells must be rectified. The intestinal wall must be allowed to rebuild itself by improving the levels of good intestinal flora in the gut.

If, having followed the regime outlined in this book for a few months, you are still having problems, then an allergy test may be necessary. It is always possible that you are reacting to one of the foods you are still eating. Be aware, however, that the body's response to foods can vary according to how the individual is feeling. When sick or under stress the body will react to more foods than when it is well. It is, therefore, essential in the long term to concentrate on building health.

Foods which caused problems can eventually be reintroduced, but this should be done gradually once health has been regained. If you introduce them too soon you may find that you react to them more strongly than you did before. This is because, having removed them from the body, it has lost its ability to adapt or cope. Do not worry about this, and continue working on improving your health; they will eventually be accepted. Never introduce more than one food at a time and do not overeat new foods, even if you can tolerate them.

ME (MYALGIC ENCEPHALOMYELITIS) AND TTT (TIRED ALL THE TIME)

ME is not always what it seems to be. Those who accept that it exists are usually looking to blame a virus. However, the virus is irrelevant as many people with ME symptoms do not have a virus present, and many with the virus present are fit and healthy. Many individuals with ME are sick because their immune systems have been weakened, allowing them to be prey to any virus which comes along. It is no use trying to find the magic bullet which will kill the virus but rather a matter of looking at why the immune system has been compromised and working at strengthening it. *Candida* weakens the body and the immune system, and many ME sufferers have *Candida* present. The body and immune system can also be weakened by stress, by poor nutrition and by general toxicity, whether it be from a toxic-laden diet, drug abuse or environmental pollution. Antibiotic overuse and vaccinations are frequent forerunners of ME symptoms.

ME has been referred to as 'yuppie flu', and it is no coincidence that ambitious over-achievers are susceptible to the problem. Like most ME sufferers, they have been living on adrenalin and pushing their bodies for too long. They may get up feeling tired, but once into the swing of the day, the adrenalin starts to flow and they feel fine. Later, when the energy flags, a game of squash or a three-mile jog gives their adrenal glands another kick and they are ready for a busy evening. Add to this the type of lifestyle that many young people live – eating too much junk food, missing meals, partaking of alcohol, taking the pill, taking antibiotics for infections – and you can see how eventually the body must give in. The mother who works, or the overstressed businessman, may not have the glamorous lifestyle of the yuppie, but the effects of living on adrenalin are the same. ME is not a disease but a series of symptoms which the body is using as a signal to let the individual know that all is not well. In fact, everything is exhausted.

ME can be seen at one end of the scale in individuals who generally do not feel well, but cope each day with a multitude of minor health problems and a continual lack of energy. They struggle by living on adrenalin and pushing their bodies to keep going. These individuals are on the verge of ME, and it takes only a strong antibiotic from the doctor, a dose of flu or a severely stressful situation to push them over the edge. At the other end of the scale are those ME sufferers who are so sick and weak they can barely stand up. They may ache from head to toe, find it impossible to think or concentrate, feel permanently sick or dizzy, and will have many more individual symptoms.

In order to recover from ME, work needs to be done on raising the blood sugar levels. This relieves some of the symptoms which are due to low blood sugar *(see page 14)* and takes pressure off the exhausted adrenal glands. The dietary regime outlined in this book is ideal for this. ME is similar to *Candida* in that it cannot be treated as an isolated problem without the individual being taken into consideration. Work needs to be done on detoxifying the body and replacing lost minerals in an attempt to repair and support all the organs, glands and systems which have become implicated. The issue of self-worth needs consideration because a lack of self-worth is frequently the motivator for overachievement *(see below).*

EMOTIONS, ADDICTIONS AND ILL HEALTH

Addictions are very common in our society and range from the more acceptable ones, such as sugar or chocolate addictions, to the more severe drug and alcohol based ones. In between is a range which includes, among many others, addictive spending, smoking, gambling, sex and shoplifting.

What each of these addictions does is to make us feel better temporarily. The fact that the consequences might be injurious to us is irrelevant at the time; we know that we will feel better if we have a chocolate bar, find a new lover, buy ourselves a new stereo or have a drink, but what we are actually doing is avoiding facing the reality of our situation. When we come down from the high that addictions create, we often feel worse than before. Unless individuals find the reasons why they are addicted they will not recover, or they will swap one addiction for another.

Within each of us is a male and female side of our personality – the animus and anima *(see chart, page 21).* The animus or male psyche used positively is responsible for drive, ambition, determination, self-reliance and discipline. The female anima used positively is responsible for feelings, emotions, intuition, softness and caring.

We are all born with different personalities. Some females have a strong animus or male side and would not be happy staying at home. They want to be out there in the world of work. Similarly, some men who have a strong anima to contend with are not assertive enough to work in the world of business but are happy in the caring professions or at home with the children. What is important is that we learn to be true to ourselves and find our own balance between the anima and animus. If, however, we have been brought up to suppress one side of our personality or

ANIMA (female psyche)
POSITIVE ASPECTS
Learning to love oneself
Learning to accept oneself
Being aware of one's needs
Learning to give to oneself
Learning to say 'no'

ANIMA
NEGATIVE ASPECTS
Illness
Doing nothing – can't get started
Addictions:
smoking
alcohol
food
men/women
sex
drugs
spending
shop-lifting
gambling

PENDULUM

NEED TO BECOME AWARE OF NEGATIVE ASPECTS OF ANIMUS AND REPLACE WITH POSITIVE ASPECTS OF ANIMA

THIS WILL ENABLE ONE TO USE THE POSITIVE ASPECTS OF THE ANIMUS

AND NOT NEED THE NEGATIVE ASPECTS OF THE ANIMA

ANIMUS (male psyche)
NEGATIVE ASPECTS
Workaholic
Compulsive
Pushing self too hard
Perfectionism
Expecting self to be superman/woman
Self-denial
I should/I shouldn't
I'm a failure/useless

ANIMUS
POSITIVE ASPECTS
Working well
Being organized
Accomplishment
Confidence
Independence
Self-reliance
Stability
Self-discipline

The Animus and Anima Chart

overemphasize the other, then often illness or addictive behaviour takes over.

This affects mostly those individuals who have an innately strong feminine side which they have learnt to repress or hide. Those with an innately strong masculine side will fit more easily into the roles which parents and society deem acceptable.

Childhood upbringing has a lot to do with the way we are. Parents have often taught their offspring not to be selfish or acknowledge their own needs (religions may have encouraged this). This lack of self-acknowledgement may have been passed on by parents who themselves had problems. Perhaps they could not express their emotions, and in doing so inadvertently taught the child to hide its feelings, or perhaps the child received very little attention so that it only felt acknowledged when it did something exceptional. Thus it always had to drive itself hard and aim continually higher in order to gain a reward. Whatever the background, and this can be as varied as the individuals with the problems, what is unfortunately being taught is a lack of self-worth. The feminine side which enables one to love, cherish and be kind to oneself is suppressed and the masculine side is encouraged, becomes overdeveloped and expresses itself negatively. Thus, instead of working well, individuals become workaholics; instead of being self-disciplined, they become self-denying; instead of being organized, they become perfectionists. Each person finds their own way of validating their self-worth dependent on their individual talents. Others will turn this drive inwards and will just be hard on themselves – 'I'm a failure' or 'I'm useless'.

In the middle of the chart is a pendulum which will always find a person's true balance between their masculine and feminine sides. If the pendulum has swung too far to the left because an individual has been working too hard or expecting too much of themselves, then it will need to swing excessively to the right to rebalance. If they are able to compensate by being kind and giving to themselves then all will be well, but what happens if they have run out of time or have never been taught to love and nurture themselves?

Addictions and illness become an alternative that satisfies a deep yearning within the subconscious, and so after a hard day individuals may turn to food, alcohol or sex in order to try to rebalance. Similarly, being ill means that they are forced to give themselves time and attention or allow others to do this by nursing them better. The feminine side may be lived out through illness or addictions, but unless it is owned by oneself then peace, health or happiness will never be fully attained.

In order to rebalance the feminine and masculine it is first necessary for individuals to see how these two aspects of their psyche are being used in their lives. Being aware of when and how they are using the negative animus is the first step. A good way of thinking of this is a shadow self walking behind you with a whip, always pushing and tormenting and expecting more. All individuals who are ill or have addictions have far higher expectations of themselves than they do of anyone else. Once one realizes how and when the whip is being used, it is much easier not to expect oneself to be superman or superwoman.

Rebuilding the positive side of the anima is about learning to be kind to oneself, to give and to indulge. It is the process of learning to understand one's needs, to love, nurture and accept oneself despite any imperfections, and is the basis of developing real self-worth.

A good idea is to write a list of 20 positive ways to 'give to oneself'. Individuals who indulge themselves with sweets, alcohol or spending, for example, often feel really bad and are hard on themselves for doing so (the animus again). These new ways are all about invoking feelings of 'this is nice', 'this is for me', 'I deserve this'. The list will vary from person to person, for what makes one of us feel guilty and indulgent will not do the same for another. It is not the issue that is important, it is the feelings of love we invoke when we do these things that we are trying to foster. The list can include things as simple as: a pot of tea with time to sit and savour it; a lazy bath; an early night; reading; walking; looking at the view; watching the cat; buying oneself a bunch of flowers.

Some individuals may say, 'Oh, that's not me. I always buy myself presents, have an early night etc.', but often they are doing these things for the wrong reasons. Are they buying new clothes because they deserve them or because their self-worth is invested in looking good? Are they indulging in an early night because they feel they would like it or to escape from reality?

By learning to be kind to ourselves we gradually discover that we have needs and that these needs must be met if we are to stay healthy. We also learn to love ourselves sufficiently to put satisfying these needs as a priority in our life and learn sufficient self-worth to be able to say 'no' when others try to distract us. An example of this might be someone who needs their own space but has a partner and family who are clingy and always demanding attention. Rather than feeling like a bad person who must be a failure and must work harder at their marriage and relationships, this person needs to accept that this is the way they are, that freedom is one of their needs and must be satisfied.

Although this all seems very indulgent and selfish, so is being ill or addicted. It is far better to give oneself the time, attention and love now while one is still able, rather than keep denying oneself and eventually needing to be looked after. Because the male animus is overdeveloped, it is easy to turn indulgences into animus things. For instance, we may say to ourselves, 'I'm going to read my book tonight', but instead of doing it with love we do it with the whip, 'You will find time to read that book'. Suddenly it has changed from a feminine, caring action into a driving ambition. In this instance, it is better to swap what we intended doing for something else: 'Instead of the book which I'm too tired to read I'm going to have an early night'.

Eventually, we can stop the pendulum swinging so wildly and decrease our need for addictions and illness by learning to live out the positive sides of the anima and animus. Following the diet outlined in *Cooking Without* will assist in this process. Because this eating regime is designed to detoxify, it will help you to work through mental and emotional toxicity which may have caused you to use the negative expressions of the anima and animus. Individuals who have worked on themselves in this way are then able to tap into the feminine qualities of feeling and intuition to see their path in life more clearly. The new base of confidence and self-reliance which they have created by utilizing the very positive attributes of the animus will enable them to move forward along this path more easily.

Using this Book

For at least the first three months of following this eating regime, I suggest that you have six meals per day! This enables the body to obtain energy from food rather than through the release of adrenalin or from the liver's glycogen stores. The energy that comes from eating regularly will not only make you feel better but will also enable the internal organs and systems of the body to recover and remove any toxic build-up.

Food may initially have to be forced into the body at regular intervals, as individuals with low blood sugar do not always feel like eating and can even feel sick at the thought of food. Once the blood sugar has been raised by the intake of food, however, the body seems grateful and will actually start asking to be fed at regular intervals. During this phase you need to make sure that you always have a snack with you wherever you are going in order to keep topping up the blood sugar. Miss the snack and let the blood sugar fall and you will spend the rest of the day feeling under par, chasing your blood sugar but never actually catching it up.

Eventually, when the body has removed excess toxins and obtained sufficient vitamins and minerals from the improved diet, three meals per day should be adequate, with an occasional piece of fruit in between. By then the liver should be supporting the blood sugar between meals, and adrenalin can be kept for emergency situations. Your body will tell you when you are ready for this; it may be in three months' time or it may be in two years' time, depending on the state of your health when you start detoxifying. Suddenly you will find that you do not feel hungry all the time, and your body will happily last from one meal to the next.

WEIGHT CONTROL

Do not worry about putting on excess weight by eating more food more often. Provided that you are only eating the foods suggested in this book, then everything in the body will function more efficiently, including the metabolism. The result will be a loss of weight for individuals who are heavier than they need to be. Anyone who is underweight will need to eat heartily on this regime as it does not encourage weight gain. Underweight people, however, often live on nervous energy which burns up calories. Because it affects mental and emotional states, *Cooking Without* promotes relaxation and therefore encourages weight gain where necessary. The art of weight control is keeping the blood sugar stable.

ORGANIZING YOUR COOKING

Do not think that *Cooking Without* is about denying yourself food. See it, rather, as about building health – eating the right kind of food in sufficient quantities at regular intervals.

Health is like a bank balance – when we become ill we have gone into the red. Even though we are overdrawn, we still have to spend energy just to do the bare essentials each day. In order to obtain health we need to minimize the amount of energy spent whilst at the same time putting as much as possible back into the bank by feeding ourselves as well as we can. In this way we eventually return our health balance to the black and have a few reserves in store for a rainy day.

It only takes a change in attitude to put food and feeding ourselves correctly at the top of our priority list for the day, rather than at the bottom, where it fits in if there is any time left. We would not dream of jumping into the car and covering up the warning light because it was indicating that the petrol tank was empty, yet how often do we do this with our bodies? By feeding ourselves well today and every day we will have many more years when we can work, look after our families, help others, play sport and live our lives well. If we do not put the effort in now, we will run out of reserves sooner or later and become ill.

Try to organize your cooking so that you have lots of tempting dishes available when you open the fridge door. In this way you will not think about what you cannot eat but rather about what you can enjoy. Put aside a few hours once or twice a week to make quite a few dishes at the same time. If you are chopping vegetables for a casserole, you might as well chop some for a soup and a terrine at the same time. You could bake fruit and nut slices at the same time as preparing a nut roast and cornmeal bread.

When cooked, decant some of the food into the freezer for emergency situations or for use later in the week. I like to place a few individual portions in 'au gratin' dishes in the freezer, but you could just fill Tupperware dishes with larger amounts. The rest of the food can be kept in the fridge so that for the next few days you have plenty to tempt you. If you always keep some cooked brown rice (it will keep for up to three days in the fridge), you only need to rustle up a salad or cook some fresh vegetables to complete a meal.

If family members do not want to change their eating patterns to fit in with you, then try making lots of dishes as suggested above, plus a few which they like. Spread the dishes out on the table for a buffet meal, but without making a distinction between their food and yours. Eventually, they will start to accept the new regime.

MAKE THE CHANGE GRADUALLY

It is a good idea to start the new regime gradually, perhaps over a period of one to four weeks, depending on how good your diet is to start with. The body is used to coping with foods, such as meat, wheat, tea and coffee, that suppress the elimination of toxins and push them back into the cells. By removing or reducing such foods and increasing the amount of vegetables eaten, toxins are encouraged to flow out of the cells, If, however, they flow out of the cells faster than the body can eliminate them to the outside world, excess toxins float around in the bloodstream, making you feel worse rather than better. This may cause a headache, anxiety, tiredness, an upset stomach or can aggravate symptoms already present. If you feel any adverse reactions to the diet then make the change more gradual, but do not give up. Your body is probably saying, 'Thank goodness! At last I can get rid of this toxic, acid waste.'

We are so accustomed to ignoring our bodies and panicking when symptoms appear that it takes time to gain an understanding of how the body works and what it is saying. As you gain health, you will also gain confidence in your body and will no longer fear growing old or becoming ill.

VEGETARIANS

This diet is ideally suited to vegetarians. Non-vegetarian ingredients included in some recipes are optional. Omitting them will speed up the elimination process still further. If you have suddenly decided to become vegetarian, then I suggest that you change over gradually to avoid excess elimination of toxins and to allow your body to become accustomed to the change.

VITAMIN AND MINERAL SUPPLEMENTS

Nutritional supplements, especially minerals, assist the elimination of toxins from the body. It is, however, impossible in a book such as this to suggest levels suitable for all readers. If you wish to use supplements to assist the detoxification process, consult a qualified nutritional therapist (*see 'Useful Addresses', page 183*).

FLUID INTAKE

Try to drink at least three pints of filtered or bottled water each day, preferably warm or at room temperature. This will help the body to remove toxins.

DOS AND DON'TS

It is difficult to devise a dietary regime that suits everyone, hence the flexible margins in this book regarding certain foods. It is probably best to err on the side of caution and remove any suspect food for a period of time or until an improvement in health has been obtained. Removing a substance from the diet means that our bodies lose their adaptability to that food, so that if it is causing a problem, this will become more apparent when it is reintroduced. When the toxins have eventually been removed from the body, the immune system will be stronger, and foods that originally caused problems will be able to be included in the diet once again.

Meat
Meat should be eaten no more than twice a week. Choose organic produce where possible. Eat poultry and game in preference to lamb, but eat lamb in preference to beef and avoid pork. Processed and cured meats such as sausages, bacon and ham should be eliminated from the diet.

Fish
Eat fish up to three times a week, preferably a selection of oily as well as white fish. Do not eat smoked fish or reconstituted fish products, such as fishfingers, although frozen fish is acceptable if a fresh supply is unavailable. Tins of salmon, tuna, sardines and other fish can be used.

Eggs
Up to five eggs per week are acceptable, preferably free-range. If you don't eat meat or fish you may have up to seven eggs per week. Those with allergies to eggs could try using an egg replacer in baked dishes (*see 'Cooking Ingredients and Methods', page 36*).

Dairy Produce
Avoid all milk – skimmed or whole – cream and cheese. Yogurt may be acceptable if health problems are not too severe, preferably made from sheep or goat's milk. Limit yourself to two to three servings a week.

Alternative Milks

Soya milk may be used in moderation, preferably from organic soya beans but without additives such as fruit sugars. Soya yogurt can be bought or made. Do not overuse soya milk as it is quite high in fat. Almond or other nut milks can be substituted if soya is not tolerated (*see recipes*) and rice milk is now available.

Vegetables

Approximately 40 per cent of food consumed should be in the form of vegetables. Each day, aim to eat a large, varied salad and a good selection of cooked vegetables, as well as having at least two completely vegetarian days each week.

Try to vary the vegetables as much as possible and use them when in season. If possible, buy organically grown produce.

Use vegetables such as:

- carrots
- parsnips
- turnips
- swede
- beetroot
- cabbage
- Brussels sprouts
- broccoli
- cauliflower
- kale
- onions
- leeks
- celery
- French beans
- runner beans
- peas
- sweetcorn
- marrow
- courgettes
- lettuce
- Chinese leaves
- radish

- cress
- fennel
- watercress
- endive
- cucumber
- sprouted seeds

Peppers, aubergines, potatoes and tomatoes should be eaten sparingly because they contain more natural toxins than other vegetables. Limit mushrooms because they encourage overgrowth of the yeast *Candida albicans*, and spinach, because it is high in oxalic acid which binds minerals such as calcium and can lower the levels absorbed by the body.

Beans and Pulses
These are good sources of protein, especially for vegetarians, and can be included in soups, casseroles and salads.

Nuts
Avoid salted nuts and peanuts. Use in moderation as nuts are high in oil and not easy to digest. Nuts are a good source of vegetable protein. Use mainly almonds, cashews, hazelnuts and walnuts. Try nut roasts and nut butters, which can be bought in health-food shops.

Seeds
Like nuts, seeds are a good source of vegetable protein. Use sesame, sunflower and pumpkin seeds and spreads such as tahini.

Rice
Rice is the ideal food for keeping blood sugar stable whilst soaking up toxic waste from the body. Preferably use short-grain, organically grown brown rice. You can use rice without limit, but each day aim to consume between 4–10 oz (115–285 g) ($1/2$–$1^1/2$ cups) (uncooked weight).

Buckwheat, Millet and Quinoa

These grains can be used instead of or as well as rice in the form of whole grains or flakes.

Corn

Corn can be used as a thickening agent in the form of flour, for baking in the form of maize meal or as sweetcorn or popcorn. Some individuals do have allergies to corn. If this is the case, use substitutions for corn in the recipes.

Wheat

Wheat contains gluten so avoid all wheat products, such as bread, cakes, biscuits, pasta, cereals and flours, for at least three months. When wheat is reintroduced, eat it no more than once a day, preferably only three to four times a week (*see page 6*).

Rye

Like wheat, rye contains gluten and should also be avoided. When wheat is reintroduced to the diet, rye could be used as an alternative.

Barley

Barley also contains gluten so should be avoided initially. It tends to cause fewer problems than wheat and is likely only to be used in small quantities in dishes such as soups and casseroles.

Oats

Although oats also contain gluten, they are generally more easily tolerated than wheat. Avoid oats if your health is seriously below par; otherwise include them no more than once per day, but preferably only three or four times per week.

Fruit

Limit yourself to one or two fruits per day. Avoid fruit juice or substitute one small glass of fruit juice for two pieces of fruit. Limit tropical fruits and very acidic fruits such as oranges, grapefruit, plums and strawberries. Apples and pears are the best fruits to be eaten regularly. Fruit may need to be avoided in the early stages of treating *Candida albicans*.

Dried Fruit
Use in moderation, preferably unsulphurized. Avoid in the early stages of treating *Candida albicans* or if you have an intolerance to yeast or suffer from flatulence or bloating.

Sugar
Avoid all sugar, brown or white. Avoid honey, molasses, malt extract and chemical sugar replacers.

Fats and Oils
Avoid or limit hardened fats and avoid hydrogenated margarine. For spreading, use sparingly low-salt butter or a non-hydrogenated margarine (which is low in trans fatty acids). Use olive oil in any heated dishes, and sweat *(see page 44)* instead of fry whenever possible. For salad dressings, olive oil is a good choice *(see 'Fats and Oils', page 8)*.

Salt
Avoid salt completely for three to four months to allow your natural tastebuds to develop. Use potassium salt substitutes if desired, and watch out for hidden forms of salt and sodium *(see 'Salt', page 11)*.

Yeast
Avoid yeast, yeast extracts (such as Marmite), shoyu/tamari sauce, miso, vinegar, monosodium glutamate, citric acid, alcohol and stock cubes. Mushrooms, tofu and dried fruit may need to be excluded from the diet if you have a yeast intolerance or *Candida albicans* is a problem *(see 'Candida Albicans', page 13)*.

Beverages
Avoid tea, coffee, carbonated soft drinks, squashes and alcohol (for advice on fruit juice, *see page 32*). Substitute with herb teas, rooibosch tea, coffee substitutes and filtered water. Beware of

additives, such as lactose and flavourings, in alternative drinks. Check the ingredients list as some coffee substitutes contain gluten. Try to drink at least 1.5 litres (3 pints/7$^{1}/_{2}$ cups) of bottled or filtered water per day (preferably warm or at room temperature) to assist detoxification.

Tinned and Frozen Produce

Avoid the general use of tinned produce, but the occasional use of tinned tuna, tomatoes and beans, for instance, is acceptable (preferably free from added sugar and salt). Limit frozen foods. Frozen fish and meat are allowed but use fresh vegetables for most meals. A few frozen vegetables, such as sweetcorn or peas, used occasionally are acceptable as they help to make meals more interesting.

WIDENING THE RANGE OF FOODS

The length of time for which this dietary regime needs to be adhered to will depend on the severity of your health problems. You may need to follow the diet for anything from a few months to a few years. Once your health has improved, try widening the range of foods consumed, but be prepared to go back to the strict regime if you do not feel as well. When reintroducing foods, try one new food at a time to see how it affects you.

You should eventually be able to reintroduce wheat, rye, barley and oats, but I recommend that you do not include wheat more than once per day. A little milk in your barleycup or rooibosch tea is acceptable, and cottage cheese and yogurt can be eaten occasionally. Salt is needed only in the occasional soup or casserole. Miso and shoyu/tamari sauce are ideal for flavouring soups and casseroles as they have many beneficial properties. A little cider vinegar, honey, molasses and sugar-free fruit spreads can be used in moderation.

The benefits you have received from *Cooking Without* will, I hope, encourage you to make this way of eating the foundation on which to build your own, individual diet for life.

Suggested Menus

BREAKFAST

Rice porridge with cinnamon, cloves and dates.
Millet porridge with fresh fruit, nuts and seeds.
Soaked muesli with fresh fruit and soya milk.
Egg fried rice.
Scrambled eggs with cornmeal bread.

MID-MORNING

Eat a snack of rice served with fresh fruit and nuts, homemade soup or chopped vegetables. Alternatively, eat a second course for breakfast and have a piece of fresh fruit or some dried fruit and nuts mid-morning. Try fruit and nut or savoury rice slices – they are easy to pick up and eat and are delicious.

LUNCH

Try homemade soup. Follow with a large mixed salad or rice salad or try stir-fried vegetables and rice or a vegetarian savoury with salad.

MID-AFTERNOON

Eat another snack; the size will depend on how late you eat your evening meal. Eat a substantial rice snack or some fruit and nuts, rice slices or rice cakes with nut butter.

EVENING MEAL

A fish, chicken or vegetarian savoury served with a good selection of fresh vegetables and/or salad, plus a portion of rice, millet, buckwheat or quinoa and, occasionally, potatoes.

SUPPER

Try soup with rice, porridge, rice with fruit, rice slices, pear and carob delight, apple, date and nut muffins.

Eat supper if you feel hungry. If you tend to wake up feeling tired or if you are not usually hungry at breakfast-time, eating supper will help maintain your blood sugar levels overnight and enable you to eat a good breakfast. If you normally feel full of energy when you wake it is because your adrenal glands have had a rest; don't live on them, feed them!

Cooking Ingredients and Methods

BROWN RICE

Some recipes call for cooked rice, others have quantities listed for uncooked rice. If you wish to substitute one for another you should note that rice approximately doubles in weight when cooked. If, therefore, a recipe calls for 225 g (8 oz/1 cup) of uncooked rice and you already have some cooked, then substitute 455 g (16 oz/2^{1}/2 cups). Rice will keep for up to three days if stored in the fridge or it can be frozen for those emergency situations. A Tupperware rice container is useful for both sieving and storing cooked rice. Most people find their own favourite way of cooking rice; here is mine.

Cooking Brown Rice
Soak 225 g (8 oz/1 cup) short-grain brown rice in a pan with lots of cold water for approximately 10 minutes. This loosens any dirt on the rice and prevents a scum forming when it is cooking. Sieve the rice and place in a pan with 1^{1}/4 litres (2 pints/5 cups) of boiling water. Bring to the boil and simmer for 25–35 mins, depending on the type of rice. There will still be lots of water left in the pan. Pour the rice and water into a sieve and allow to drain. Serve hot or leave to cool in the sieve over the pan with the pan lid on top to prevent the rice from drying out. Long-grain brown rice does not

take as long to cook as short-grain rice, but cooking times can vary with different batches of rice.

Flavouring Brown Rice
Brown rice can be cooked in stock to add flavour. It can also be flavoured whilst cooking with herbs or spices (such as coriander, fennel or a bay leaf), or it can be cooked with the addition of onion, garlic or fresh ginger. Add more than one flavouring and produce interesting variations. Cooked rice can be flavoured by adding one or more of the following: toasted sunflower or sesame seeds, slivered almonds, grated orange or lemon rind, fresh herbs (coriander, mint, parsley), olive oil.

MILLET, BUCKWHEAT AND QUINOA

These grains can be used in recipes as an alternative to boiled rice. To cook, follow the instructions for cooking brown rice, but cook buckwheat and quinoa for approximately 10 minutes and millet for approximately 18 minutes. Try using in nut roasts, salads and rice slices. Like rice, millet doubles in weight once cooked. Buckwheat and quinoa treble in weight, so if substituting for rice in recipes, adjust accordingly.

COOKING BEANS

Cooking time depends on the age of the beans (old beans take longer), the size of the beans and the length of the soaking time. Smaller beans and pulses, such as lentils, mung beans, aduki beans and split peas, can be cooked without soaking. Larger beans need soaking overnight in plenty of water which has been brought to the boil. Discard the soaking water and rinse well before cooking. Even after soaking, large beans can take up to two hours to cook. This is where I find a pressure cooker invaluable as most large beans can be cooked in only five minutes after an overnight soak. They are not mushy at this stage but are ready to place in dishes such as casseroles and soups. Beans approximately double in size when soaked and cooked.

Beans can be frozen at the soaked stage or at the just-cooked stage so that a supply is always at hand. Try freezing them in a colander or sieve as this allows any excess water to drain away. The beans can then be tipped into a plastic bag where, with a little encouragement, they will become free flowing, allowing you to take out just the amount you need at any time.

I always keep a few tins of beans in the cupboard for those emergency situations. They do, however, contain salt so I discard the liquid and rinse well. Tinned beans do seem to be easier to digest and appear to cause less flatulence than the fresh variety.

STOCK

Stock can be made from leftover bones, fresh bones, giblets, vegetables and vegetable cooking water.

Vegetables should always be steamed or cooked in as little water as possible to prevent minerals leaching into the cooking water. However, saving any leftover cooking liquid for soup stock will add flavour and minerals to the soup. I keep a container in the ice box of my fridge, and each day add any leftover cooking water to it. When I am ready to make soup the stock is ready. Do not use stock from cauliflower or other strong-tasting vegetables as this will alter the flavour of the soup.

Bones can be obtained from most butchers, but do not use bacon bones as these contain sodium. Raw bones produce a better flavoured stock if they are roasted first in a hot oven until brown. Stock made from bones should be brought to the boil and simmered for an hour, making sure that the water level just covers the bones. A pressure cooker saves time when making stock. When cooked, sieve the stock, allow to cool and remove any fat from the surface. Try to cook stock in large quantities and freeze some so that stock is always available.

Fish stock can be made by asking the fishmonger for bones and boiling these in sufficient water to cover them for just 10 minutes. Cooking longer gives the stock a strong, bitter flavour.

SPROUTED SEEDS

Sprouts can be grown from most whole beans and pulses, but your supply needs to be fresh as old seeds do not sprout well. Some of the easiest to grow are lentils, alfalfa, mung and aduki. You can buy special trays in which to grow your seeds, but a jam jar will suffice.

Place 15 ml (1 tbsp) of the seeds in the jar and soak overnight in lots of cold water. The following morning either fasten a piece of muslin over the jam jar or use the lid to sieve the water from the seeds. Rinse the seeds in more fresh water then drain again, and this time leave to stand in a warm, preferably dark place (a dark jar can be used). Each morning and evening, rinse and drain the jar. In two to three days (depending on the warmth), you will have sprouts ready to eat. They are ready when leaves begin to appear.

ORANGE AND LEMON – JUICE AND RIND

Neither of these juices should be used in large quantities as they cause excess elimination of toxins from the cells which, if not removed by the body, can cause symptoms to appear. They are, however, ideal used in small quantities to add flavour to recipes. I keep ice cubes made from orange and lemon juice in the freezer for such occasions. Orange and lemon rind can also be frozen, but preferably buy organically grown fruit as most fruits will have been heavily sprayed. Grate and loosely pack into small containers. If you cannot tolerate citrus fruits, leave these flavourings out of recipes.

GINGER

Fresh ginger goes mouldy quite quickly even if kept in the fridge, so peel a large piece of ginger and freeze. Whenever you need ginger for a recipe, grate a little whilst it is still frozen and return the rest to the freezer.

HERBS

I like to use fresh herbs whenever possible so I grow or buy these, chop them and place in small containers in the freezer so that they are always available. If you do not have fresh or frozen herbs, substitute dried herbs, but use only one quarter of the fresh amount.

MISO

Although miso is a fermented soya product containing salt, it is such a good food nutritionally that I feel it is worth including in the diet if it can be tolerated. If you have *Candida albicans* or a yeast intolerance, you will need to avoid miso for a long period and should use it sparingly when it is eventually introduced. The salt content is approximately 8–10 per cent. Some miso contains barley or rice, so check the ingredients. Use miso in the same way as you would stock cubes by dissolving in a small amount of boiling water.

SHOYU/TAMARI SAUCE

These are fermented from soya beans, developing a deep, rich flavour that tastes saltier than it is. They are both available from health-food shops. When buying, read labels carefully as most supermarket versions contain wheat and monosodium glutamate. Avoid tamari and shoyu if you have *Candida albicans* or a yeast intolerance.

SEAWEEDS

Although seaweeds do contain salt, wash well and use whenever possible in soups, casseroles and salads as seaweed is a very good natural source of vitamins and minerals.

MUSTARD

This is not an easy product to find without added vinegar or wheat but it is available as mustard flour with no other added ingredients and as an English mustard with only salt added *(see 'Useful Addresses', page 183)*.

VINEGAR SUBSTITUTES

Use the equivalent amount of lemon juice or try powdered vitamin C instead of vinegar – 2 ml ($^1/_4$ tsp) for each 15 ml (1 tbsp) of vinegar.

OLIVES

Most olives seem to be preserved in brine but you can buy olives in olive oil from some delicatessens. Some preservatives contain other additives, such as citric acid, which need to be avoided. Because olives are used only in small quantities and give a wonderful flavour to dishes, I accept the small amount of additional salt. I just wash them well.

TOMATOES

If you cannot tolerate tomatoes but can use miso or tamari, then use these in recipes instead of tomato purée. Where a tin or carton of tomato juice is listed in the ingredients, substitute carrot or other vegetable juices.

SUN-DRIED TOMATOES

These are available bottled in olive oil although many seem to contain vinegar or citric acid (check labels). I have, however, found sun-dried tomatoes in a packet with no additives. These need soaking in water to soften.

PASTA

This is available made from ingredients such as rice, cornmeal and buckwheat instead of wheat. Spelt, from which some lasagne and pastas are now being made, is derived from an ancient wheat grain, and although it is not gluten free, it seems to cause fewer problems than modern wheats.

EGG REPLACERS

Egg replacers can be used to bind ingredients together but will not help a mixture to rise. These are readily available in health-food shops. Alternatively, an egg replacer can be made by simmering together for five minutes 15 ml (1 tbsp) of flax seeds (which can be bought as Linusit Gold) and 115 ml (4 fl oz/^{1}/$_2$ cup) of water. This will produce a mixture which is the consistency of raw egg white and equates to one egg. You do not need to strain the mixture as the flax seeds will just add fibre to your recipe.

PUFFED RICE CAKES

These are often used as a substitute for bread, and there is no problem with this except that rice cakes contain mainly air and very little rice. Do not use unless accompanied by a substantial meal.

THICKENERS

Cornflour has been used as a thickening agent in some recipes. Other flours can be substituted but the amount used may need to be adjusted. To thicken 425 ml (^{3}/$_4$ pint/2 cups) of liquid use one of the following:

vel tbsp) potato flour
el tbsp) rice flour or cornflour
el tbsp) gram flour, soya flour or cornmeal

RAISING AGENTS

Ordinary baking powder is not acceptable because of its sodium base. Potassium baking powder is available in health-food shops (ask if you cannot see it). Use as you would ordinary baking powder.

FOOD FAMILIES

Individuals with severe allergies or intolerances may find that foods related to the ones to which they are intolerant can also cause problems. Ignore the list below unless you are still having trouble with your diet after six months, in which case it may be worth avoiding the foods related to your problem foods:

Banana ginger, tumeric, cardamom.

Beet chard, spinach, sugar (beet), beetroot.

Carrot caraway, celery, chervil, coriander, cumin, dill, fennel, parsley, parsnip, celeriac.

Cashew mango, pistachio.

Compositae lettuce, chicory, sunflower, safflower, dandelion, camomile, artichoke.

Grasses wheat, corn, barley, oats, millet, cane sugar, bamboo shoots, rice, rye (buckwheat is not a member of the grass family).

Legume beans, lentils, liquorice, peas, senna, soya, string beans.

Mustard broccoli, Brussels sprouts, cabbage, Chinese leaves, cauliflower, cress, horseradish, kale, kohlrabi, radish, swede, turnip, watercress, rapeseed.

Palm coconut, date, sago.

Potato aubergine, pepper, chilli, tobacco, tomato, cape gooseberry.

Rose apple, pear, apricot, cherry, peach, plum, blackberry, raspberry, strawberry.

Equipment

Do not cook with aluminium pans, as aluminium is a toxic metal. Non-stick pans have similar problems. Pressure cookers are usually made of aluminium but are available in stainless steel.

A food processor is a labour-saving piece of equipment. It can be used for slicing, chopping or shredding vegetables and it will also liquidize, purée and mix. If a food processor is not available then, in many instances, a liquidizer or blender can be used.

General Information

I have tried to include alternative ingredients in many instances, but this is not always possible without making recipes excessively long. Most recipes, however, will adapt to substitutions. Vegetables can be exchanged in recipes, and alternative flours can be used in baking. Egg substitutes can be used in most recipes, and nut or rice milk can be used instead of soya milk. Ingredients used to add flavour, such as tomato purée, orange juice or lemon rind, can be omitted.

Sweating is used in quite a few recipes to impart more flavour. This is not the same as frying as the temperatures used are much lower. It involves softening the vegetables in oil until they begin to brown, but it does take time. Allow at least 20 minutes, and sweat vegetables whilst you collect other ingredients together to save time.

Folding is used in a few recipes and involves mixing ingredients using a metal spoon and following a figure-of-eight movement. This prevents the air being beaten out of the ingredients.

I have kept oven temperatures the same in many recipes so that you can bake several dishes at the same time.

Breakfast

Breakfast is a very important meal. First thing in the morning, we are literally breaking our night's fast. If you have difficulty eating breakfast or feel sick at the thought of it, this means that your blood sugar has dropped too low overnight. Start by eating small amounts of breakfast, perhaps fruit or something light to start with, and gradually increase this amount until a substantial breakfast is not only acceptable but actually desired.

It is occasionally necessary for some people to eat in the middle of the night to prevent the blood sugar dropping so low. When toxicity has eventually been removed and sufficient minerals have been obtained, blood sugar levels will be stable for longer periods. If the blood sugar is not raised by breakfast first thing in the morning, then people often spend all day chasing it but never achieving stability or feeling good, however much they eat.

If you like to lie in at the weekend, take your breakfast to bed with you. Set the alarm as normal, eat your breakfast and go back to sleep, making sure that you are up before your mid-morning snack. If you normally feel worse after a lie-in, it is because your blood sugar levels have dropped too low by the time you eat.

Although I have tried to make the recipes in this section conform to typical breakfast dishes, what you eat for breakfast does not really matter as long as it raises your blood sugar. Some breakfast dishes could be used for meals and snacks during the day, such as Bubble and Squeak for lunch or Pear and Carob Delight as a pudding or supper dish. Other breakfast suggestions include breads from Chapter 9, Rice Pudding *(see page 170)*, Kedgeree *(see page 139)* and eggs, boiled, scrambled or poached.

As all the recipes are gluten-free, they exclude oats, a delicious breakfast cereal. I have noted where oats can be substituted for those who do not have a problem with gluten. Millet flakes have a distinctive flavour which takes some adjusting to, as do buckwheat flakes which can be used instead of or as well as millet flakes. Linseeds (available in health-food shops) have many health-giving properties *(see 'Fats and Oils', Introduction, page 8)* and are ideal to sprinkle on breakfast cereals. Store them in an airtight container in the fridge and add 10 ml (1 dsp) to breakfast cereals before serving.

If dried fruit cannot be tolerated because of *Candida albicans* or a yeast intolerance, then omit it from these recipes and use fresh fruit in its place. Some individuals may be able to tolerate crystallized pineapple and ginger or dried apple better than dried fruit. Although ginger and pineapple do contain some sugar, the amounts used are small and they may help to make an unacceptable dish more agreeable for some people.

When cup measurements *only* are given, I use a tea cup but the size does not matter as long as you keep the proportions the same.

MUESLI

Oat flakes can be substituted for the millet flakes if gluten can be tolerated. Vary the fruit and nuts so that each muesli you make is different, for example, hazelnut and apricot, raisin and almond or mixed fruit and nut. If you cannot tolerate dried fruit, serve the muesli with fresh fruit, either raw or stewed.

7 cups millet flakes	½ cup sunflower seeds
1 cup nuts	1 cup coconut flakes or ¼ cup
1 cup dried fruit (optional)	desiccated coconut

1 Mix all the ingredients together and store in a container.
2 Serve with soya, almond or rice milk and fresh fruit.

LIGHT MUESLI

Oats can be substituted for the millet flakes if gluten can be tolerated. Serve with fresh fruit if dried fruit is not allowed.

4 cups puffed rice cereal
½ cup sunflower seeds
¾ cup mixed dried fruit
  e.g. chopped dates, apricots,
  figs, raisins or sultanas (optional)

¾ cup mixed nuts
4 cups millet flakes
½ cup desiccated coconut

1 Mix all the ingredients together and store in a container.
2 Serve with soya, almond or rice milk.

MILLET PORRIDGE

Oat porridge can be made in the same way for those who can tolerate oats.

Ingredients per person:

1 cup millet flakes   2¾ cups cold water

1 Place the ingredients in a pan and bring to the boil, stirring.
2 Simmer gently for approximately 10 minutes.
3 Serve plain with soya, almond or rice milk or with fresh fruit, dried fruit, nuts and seeds piled on top. These could be added to the porridge whilst it is cooking to vary the recipe.

SOAKED MUESLI

This muesli is ideal to take on holiday as it can be easily made up in hotel bedrooms and can also be used for between-meal snacks. My favourite version of this recipe contains 55 g (2 oz/½ cup) of crystallized pineapple instead of 55 g (2 oz/½ cup) of the raisins, and I use whole almonds for the nuts. Oats can be substituted for the millet flakes if gluten is allowed. Serve with fresh fruit if dried fruit is not tolerated.

---

340 g (12 oz/3 cups) rice flakes	115 g (4 oz/1 cup) raisins or
255 g (9 oz/3 cups) millet flakes	mixed dried fruit (optional)
55 g (2 oz/½ cup) sunflower seeds	55 g (2 oz/½ cup) nuts

1 Mix all the ingredients together and store in an airtight container.
2 Fill a breakfast bowl with the muesli and soak in sufficient water just to cover the ingredients. Allow to stand for at least 15 minutes or, if desired, soak overnight.
3 Serve with soya, almond or rice milk, soya yogurt or just as it is.

RICE PORRIDGE

Rice flakes vary a lot in the amount of water they soak up, so adjust the liquid accordingly.

Ingredients per person:

1 cup brown rice flakes	2 ml (¼ tsp) cinnamon
1 ml (⅛ tsp) ground cloves	2½ cups boiling water
1 piece fresh fruit	10 ml (1 dsp) dried fruit
e.g. apple, pear, banana	e.g. raisins, dates (optional)

1 Place all the ingredients except the fresh fruit into a pan, bring to the boil and simmer gently for 10 minutes, stirring occasionally.
2 Cut the fresh fruit into pieces and add to the pan 2 minutes before the end of cooking or pile on top just before serving.

BREAKFAST RICE

1 bowl of cooked rice per person plus a selection from the following:

- nuts and seeds
- desiccated coconut
- spices e.g. nutmeg
- soya milk, rice milk, fruit juice or soya yogurt
- finely diced dried fruit
- stewed dried fruit
- chopped fresh fruit

- stewed fresh fruit
- carob powder

It is a good idea to keep toppings such as nuts, seeds, toasted nuts and seeds and chopped dried fruit in clear glass jars on your work surface or shelf. Then you can quickly add toppings to a bowl of warm or cold rice. Children love the idea of helping themselves to toppings.

Suggested combinations for 1 bowl of rice:

- ½ chopped banana, a few cashew nuts or raisins.
- ½ stewed apple, pinch cinnamon, toasted sunflower seeds.
- ½ pear, chopped dried apricots, toasted slivered almonds.
- Liquidize ½ peach and ½ banana and pour over the rice.
- Stewed prunes and soya yogurt.
- Stewed dried apricots and chopped almonds.
- ½ pear, nutmeg and warm soya milk.
- 5 ml (1 tsp) carob flour, pinch nutmeg and warm soya milk.

PEAR AND CAROB DELIGHT

A banana can be substituted for the pear in this recipe.

Ingredients per person:

40 ml (2 rounded tbsp) rice flour
170 ml (6 fl oz/¾ cup) soya,
    rice or almond milk
170 ml (6 fl oz/¾ cup) boiling water

10 ml (1 dsp) carob flour
1 small pear
10 ml (1 dsp) desiccated coconut

1 In a pan mix the rice and carob flour to a smooth paste with a little milk. Gradually add the remaining milk.
2 Cut the pear into thin slices and add to the pan with the coconut.
3 Add the boiling water and bring the mixture to the boil, stirring.
4 Lower the heat and simmer for 5–10 minutes or until the pear begins to disintegrate, sweetening the mixture.

BANANA AND MAIZE BREAKFAST CEREAL

If desired, a piece of vanilla pod can be used instead of the extract, and a pear can be substituted for the banana.

Ingredients per person:

40 ml (2 rounded tbsp) maize meal
2 drops natural vanilla extract
170 ml (6 fl oz/¾ cup) boiling water

170 ml (6 fl oz/¾ cup) soya, rice or almond milk
1 small banana

1 Mix the maize meal to a smooth paste with the milk in a pan.
2 Add the vanilla extract, the boiling water and the finely sliced banana.
3 Bring the mixture to the boil, stirring constantly.
4 Lower the heat and simmer for 5–10 mins or until the banana begins to disintegrate.

SAGO BREAKFAST CEREAL

If desired, a piece of vanilla pod can be used instead of the extract. Sago does seem to vary in the amount of liquid it absorbs. Adjust the recipe if necessary.

Ingredients per person:

40 ml (2 rounded tbsp) sago
½ banana or pear, chopped
200 ml (7 fl oz/¾ cup) soya or almond milk
2 drops natural vanilla extract

200 ml (7 fl oz/¾ cup) boiling water
10 ml (1 dsp) finely chopped dates (optional)

1 Place all the ingredients into a pan, bring to the boil, stirring constantly, then lower the heat.
2 Simmer for 15–20 minutes, stirring occasionally.
3 The fruit should begin to disintegrate, sweetening the mixture.

SOYA MILK YOGURT

The mixture ideally needs to fill a flask in order for the yogurt to stay warm. Adjust the quantities if your flask is larger.

Yogurt culture can be bought to use as a starter or use 5 ml (1 tsp) of a bought soya yogurt. Even though these normally contain some sugar there will be very little in the amount used. The yogurt will not take as long to set if using soya yogurt or a culture.

570 ml (1 pint/2½ cups) organic soya milk
4 milk-free acidophilus capsules

1 Bring the milk to the boil and then allow to cool to body temperature (a clean finger is sufficient to test). Cover the pan to prevent a skin forming.
2 Empty the acidophilus capsules into a small basin and add 1 tsp of the warm soya milk, mixing until you have a smooth paste. Continue adding the soya milk and mixing until the acidophilus is well blended, then pour into the pan and stir.
3 Pour the mixture into a warmed vacuum flask, put the top on and leave to stand for approximately 6 hours or until the mixture just starts to leave the sides of the flask when the flask is tipped.
4 Tip the yogurt out into a container and store in the fridge.

ALMOND MILK

Other nuts, such as cashews, can be used instead of almonds. The milk will keep for 48 hours in the fridge but will separate a little on standing. Shake before using.

½ cup blanched almonds   2¼ cups water

1 To blanch the almonds, pour boiling water over the nuts and leave them to stand for 5 minutes. The skins should then easily slip off when pressed with the thumb.
2 Place the nuts in a blender and blend until finely ground.

3 Add ½ cup of water and blend until a smooth cream is formed.
4 Add the remaining water and blend well.
5 Put the mixture through a fine sieve. If there is a great deal of pulp left, you have not blended for long enough.

BREAKFAST IN A GLASS

Try substituting other fresh fruits such as peaches, apricots and mango, or add 5 ml (1 tsp) carob powder to the banana.

1 banana or other soft fruit	40 ml (2 heaped tbsp) cooked rice
pinch nutmeg	90 ml (3 fl oz/⅓ cup) soya, almond or rice milk

1 Place all the ingredients in a food processor and liquidize until smooth.
2 Pour the mixture into a glass and eat as you would a yogurt.

MARMALADE

2 oranges (preferably organic) *or* 1 orange and 1 lemon
225 g (8 oz/1¼ cups) dried apricots, cut into pieces
140 ml (5 fl oz/⅔ cup) water

1 Wash the oranges well and squeeze the juice from them.
2 Place the juice in a pan along with the apricot pieces.
3 Bring the apricots and juice to the boil, lower the heat, place a lid on the pan and simmer for approximately 10 minutes or until the apricots are soft. Add a little water if the mixture starts to become too dry. The amount of water needed and the length of cooking time will be determined by how old the apricots are.
4 Cut the peel from the oranges into matchstick-size pieces and place in a pan along with the water.
5 Bring to the boil and simmer for 10 minutes or until the peel is soft.
6 Process the apricots and juice to form a soft, smooth purée.

7 Mix together the apricot purée, the orange peel and any juices from the pan. Add a little more liquid if the mixture is too stiff.

8 Allow to cool. Place the marmalade into two jars or containers. I suggest you store one in the fridge where it will keep for up to two weeks and the other in the freezer.

FRUIT SPREAD

Fruit spreads can be made by stewing and liquidizing fresh or dried fruit. Do not include the cooking liquid as this will make the spread too runny. If the spread is still too soft, thicken with a little arrowroot or Gelozone (the vegetarian equivalent of gelatine, available in health-food shops and some supermarkets). Try apple and cinnamon, dried apricot or mixed summer fruits. The spreads will not keep for more than a few days if made with fresh fruit.

EGG FRIED RICE (SERVES 4)

15 ml (1 tbsp) of shoyu/tamari sauce will add extra flavour (if it is allowed). Try serving with a salad for lunch.

4 eggs	80 ml (8 dsp) water
10 ml (1 dsp) olive oil	455 g (1 lb/2 ^{2}/3 cups)
black pepper	cooked rice

1 Beat the eggs with 4 dsp water.

2 Pour 5 ml (1 tsp) of oil into a frying pan, heat and add the eggs. Cook as an omelette by lifting the edges of the mixture as it cooks and allowing any uncooked mixture to run to the base.

3 Cut the omelette into little pieces either in the pan or by removing and cutting on a chopping board.

4 Place the cooked egg and rice into the pan along with 5 ml (1 tsp) of oil and the black pepper. Stir-fry until heated through.

5 Add the remaining 4 dsp water and allow this to be absorbed, then serve.

SCRAMBLED TOFU WITH SWEETCORN AND ARAME (SERVES 4)

Use 10 ml (1 dsp) of water in the pan if you prefer not to fry. 10 ml (1 dsp) of shoyu/tamari sauce can be added (if it is allowed).

80 ml (4 tbsp) arame seaweed	5 ml (1 tsp) olive oil
225 g (8 oz/1¼ cups) sweetcorn kernels	225 g (8 oz/2 cups) tofu, plain or smoked

1 Soak the arame in boiling water for approximately 10 minutes or until soft. Sieve to remove the water.
2 Place the olive oil in a pan then add the arame, the sweetcorn and the tofu crumbled into tiny pieces.
3 Warm through by stir-frying, and serve.

RICE WITH LEEKS AND SCRAMBLED EGGS (SERVES 4)

455 g (1 lb/4 cups) leeks, chopped	455 g (1 lb/2⅔ cups) cooked rice
6 eggs	
black pepper	

1 Cook the leeks in a little water until just tender. Drain well.
2 Warm the rice if not freshly cooked.
3 Beat the eggs with 45 ml (3 tbsp) of water and scramble.
4 Mix all the ingredients together and season with black pepper.

POTATO CAKES (SERVES 4)

Try substituting parsnips for the potatoes if these cause a problem.

680 g (1½ lb/5 cups) potatoes	60 ml (3 rounded tbsp) rice flour
black pepper	extra flour for shaping
15 ml (1 tbsp) olive oil	

1 Peel, chop and cook the potatoes in boiling water until soft.
2 Sieve and keep the liquid. Mash the potatoes until smooth using a little of the cooking liquid to moisten.
3 Add the rice flour and pepper and mix well.
4 Take handfuls of the mixture and roll into balls using rice flour to keep the mixture from sticking to your hands. Flatten the balls into cakes approximately 1½ cm (½ inch) thick.
5 Fry the cakes in a little oil until they begin to brown (approximately 5 minutes). Turn and fry the other side. Serve spread with butter if allowed or to accompany other breakfast dishes.

TRADITIONAL ENGLISH BREAKFAST (SERVES 4)

Try to buy organic kidneys or liver and soak overnight in a little soya milk if you prefer a less strong flavour. Baked beans bought from a health-food shop may be acceptable but check the ingredients first.

4 whole kidneys	olive oil and black pepper
or 4 pieces lamb's liver	4–8 potato cakes
4 beef tomatoes	4 eggs
340 g (12 oz/3 cups) mushrooms	

1 Cut the kidneys in half, skin them and remove the core. Brush the kidneys or liver with oil and sprinkle with black pepper. Grill for approximately 5 minutes on each side under a medium heat until they are cooked.
2 Cut the tomatoes in half, sprinkle with black pepper and place under the grill with the kidneys 2 minutes before the end of cooking. Warm the potato cakes in a similar way.
3 Wash and chop the mushrooms and fry in a little oil until just cooked.
4 Scramble or poach the eggs according to your preference.
5 Assemble the ingredients on 4 warm plates.

SWEETCORN AND ONION FRITTERS (SERVES 4)

Try substituting other vegetables and beans in this recipe, such as peas and white cabbage or butterbeans and green peppers.

1 large onion, finely chopped
70 g (2½ oz/⅓ cup) rice flour
285 ml (10 fl oz/1 ⅓ cup) water
15 ml (1 tbsp) fresh parsley
olive oil

115 g (4 oz/⅔ cup) sweetcorn
 kernels
1 large egg, beaten
black pepper

1 Cook the onion in 30 ml (2 tbsp) water until soft. Drain.
2 Place the sweetcorn kernels in a bowl and roughly mash with the back of a fork until the kernels are just broken.
3 Add the onion, rice flour, water, egg, parsley and black pepper to the sweetcorn. Mix well.
4 Fry as two large pancakes in the olive oil until the pancakes are set and golden brown, turning half-way through cooking *(see the 'Bubble and Squeak' recipe below for how to turn).*

BUBBLE AND SQUEAK (SERVES 4)

Ideally, make this dish with leftover potatoes and cabbage for a quick breakfast dish. Other leftover vegetables could be substituted for the cabbage (such as carrots, peas and beans) and parsnips could be substituted for the potatoes if these cause problems.

680 g (1½ lb/5 cups) potatoes
black pepper
15 ml (1 tbsp) olive oil

225 g (8 oz/4 cups) white
 cabbage

1 Cook the potatoes in boiling water until soft.
2 Chop and cook the cabbage, preferably steamed over the potatoes. Do not over-cook.

3 Mash the potatoes with a little of the cooking water until soft and smooth. Add the cabbage and pepper and mix well.
4 Grease a frying pan with half of the olive oil and fry the potato mixture flattened into a pancake shape for approximately 10 minutes or until crisp and brown.
5 Slide the mixture out of the pan onto a chopping board, cooked side downwards. Grease the pan with the remaining oil and invert the pan over the potato mixture. Lift both the pan and the chopping board and turn over so that the mixture tips into the frying pan with the uncooked side downwards.
6 Cook for a further 10 minutes or until the second side is brown.

POTATO PANCAKES (SERVES 2–4)

1 egg, beaten
140 ml (5 fl oz/^{2}/$_3$ cup) water
1 small onion, grated
10 ml (1 dsp) chopped fresh parsley or other fresh herbs

55 g (2 oz/^{1}/$_3$ cup) rice flour
255 g (9 oz/2 cups) grated raw potato
15 ml (1 tbsp) olive oil

1 Mix all the ingredients together, except the oil.
2 Fry as one large pancake in half of the oil for approximately 15 minutes, turning the heat down low after the first few minutes to prevent burning. Turn the pancake and fry in the remaining oil for a further 15 minutes. The outside of the pancake should be crisp and golden and the potatoes cooked through on the inside.

Starters

Starters can be used as snacks, light lunches or suppers. If you normally have a two-course evening meal involving a pudding, try serving a starter instead so that you avoid the pudding trap. Puddings can then be saved for weekends.

Many of the salads in Chapter 4 can be served as starters. Try minted avocado and chickpeas or curried egg and rice served on a bed of lettuce. If you do not like main-course salads, then serve a salad starter to benefit from eating more raw vegetables.

STUFFED LETTUCE LEAVES (SERVES 4)

Those allowed could use cottage cheese instead of tofu and serve with crusty bread to mop up the juices. Prawns contain salt unless freshly boiled. Avocado can be substituted for the eggs.

8 large soft lettuce leaves	cress to garnish
French dressing to serve (see Chapter 8, page 143)	

Stuffing:

55 g (2 oz/½ cup) prawns	2 hardboiled eggs
40 ml (2 tbsp) mayonnaise	40 ml (2 tbsp) grated tofu
15 g (½ oz/⅙ cup) ground almonds	15 ml (1 tbsp) fresh herbs
2 ml (¼ tsp) grated lemon rind	e.g. parsley, mint, chives

1 Finely chop the eggs and the herbs, then mix all the stuffing ingredients together.
2 Divide the stuffing mixture between the eight lettuce leaves, roll up and place two leaves on each plate.
3 Garnish with the cress and serve with French dressing.

Variations

Lettuce leaves can be stuffed with a selection of finely chopped or grated vegetables mixed with sufficient mayonnaise or yogurt to bind, such as avocado, tomato, pepper, spring onions (scallions), carrot, cucumber, sweetcorn, sprouted seeds. Some brown rice could be included.

SPINACH AND CARROT TIMBALE
(SERVES 4–6)

This is a delicious dish to serve as a vegetarian main course along with Fresh Tomato Sauce *(see Chapter 8, page 147)*. Other vegetables could be substituted, such as parsnips for the carrots, and leeks or cauliflower instead of the spinach.

455 g (1 lb /8 cups) spinach
2 ml (¼ tsp) nutmeg
1 egg
1 clove garlic

455g (1 lb/3 cups) carrots
black pepper
sliced tomato and toasted
 sesame seeds to garnish

1 Cook the spinach (in the water which remains on the leaves after washing) for no more than 5 minutes. Drain.
2 Cut the carrots into even sized pieces and cook until just tender.
3 Purée the carrots with a little of the cooking liquid, the nutmeg and some black pepper.
4 Process the spinach with the egg, the garlic and lots of black pepper until a smooth purée is formed.
5 Place a layer of carrot purée, then a layer of spinach purée, into 4 gratin or 6 ramekin dishes.
6 Cover with foil and bake at 400°F/200°C/gas mark 6 for 10–15 minutes or until the spinach purée has set.
7 Garnish with sliced tomatoes and toasted sesame seeds.

WARM CHICKEN LIVER SALAD (SERVES 4)

Use coarse-grain mustard and organic chicken livers if possible. If allowed, add a knob of butter to the oil and mop up the juices with some crusty bread.

115 g (4 oz/1 ⅓ cups) continental salad leaves e.g. frisee, radicchio, lamb's lettuce (corn salad)

2 cloves garlic
225 g (8 oz/1 cup) chicken livers
10 ml (1 dsp) olive oil
5 ml (1 tsp) mustard

1 Wash the leaves and arrange on 4 serving plates.
2 Crush the garlic cloves and cut the chicken livers into small pieces.
3 Heat the oil in a frying pan, add the garlic and cook for a few seconds before adding the chicken livers. Fry quickly until the livers begin to brown and are just cooked.
4 Add the mustard and mix in.
5 Spoon the hot livers onto the salad, including any juices from the pan. Serve immediately.

AVOCADO DIP (SERVES 4)

Serve as a dip with vegetable crudités or as a pâté with rice cakes and a salad garnish. If desired, 15 ml (1 tbsp) of mayonnaise can be added.

1 clove garlic (optional)
15 ml (1 tbsp) olive oil
pinch chilli powder
black pepper

2 ripe avocados
10 ml (1 dsp) lemon juice
3 ml (½ tsp) paprika

1 Press the garlic clove and place in a bowl with the rest of the ingredients.
2 Mash with a fork to give a rough textured dip.

AVOCADO AND CASHEW NUT PÂTÉ (SERVES 4)

Butter beans could be used instead of the eggs, and other nuts could replace the cashew nuts.

1 ripe medium avocado
55 g (2 oz/½ cup) cashew nuts
15 ml (1 tbsp) fresh parsley
2 hardboiled eggs

15 ml (1 tbsp) lemon juice
1–2 spring onions (scallions)
4 black olives (optional)
black pepper

1 Mash the avocado and lemon juice with a fork.
2 Toast the cashew nuts, finely grind and allow to cool.
3 Finely chop the spring onion (scallion), parsley, olives and hardboiled eggs by hand.
4 Mix all the ingredients together. Add a little water or soya milk if a softer pâté is required or if you wish to turn the pâté into a dip.
5 Serve with rice cakes, bread, vegetable crudités, salad etc.

CARROT AND APRICOT PÂTÉ (SERVES 4–6)

85 g (3 oz/½ cup) dried apricots
85 g (3 oz/⅓ cup) grated tofu
black pepper
30 g (1 oz/⅓ cup) ground almonds
15 ml (1 tbsp) lemon juice

90 ml (3 fl oz/⅓ cup) water
2 ml (⅓ tsp) cardamom
2 ml (¼ tsp) nutmeg
225 g (8 oz/1 ⅓ cups)
    grated carrot

1 Cut the dried apricots into small pieces. Place in the water and simmer for 10 minutes or until soft.
2 Mix all the ingredients together by hand including any liquid remaining with the apricots.
3 Place in a small greased loaf tin, cover and bake for 45 mins at 400°F/200°C/gas mark 6.
4 Cool a little, cut into slices and serve with a salad and rice cakes.

CARROT AND CASHEW NUT PÂTÉ
(SERVES 4–6)

Serve on rice cakes with a salad garnish or as a sandwich spread. For a variation, if allowed, add 40 ml (2 tbsp) cottage cheese and mix well.

255 g (9 oz/1 ⅔ cups) carrots, sliced
5 ml (1 tsp) chopped mint
15 ml (1 tbsp) chopped chives
   or spring onion (scallion)
black pepper

115 g (4 oz/1 cup) cashew nuts
3 ml (½ tsp) grated orange rind
approx. 15 ml (1 tbsp) orange
   juice or soya milk

1 Slice and then cook the carrots in a little water until just soft. Sieve and cool.
2 Place the cashew nuts in a food processor and process until finely ground.
3 Add the carrots, mint, orange rind, onions or chives and pepper and process again. If necessary, add a little orange juice or milk to obtain a smooth pâté.

BUTTERBEAN, TUNA AND MINT PÂTÉ
(SERVES 4–6)

1 tin (200 g/7 oz/1⅓ cups)
   tuna in water
15 ml (1 tbsp) olive oil
5 ml (1 tsp) fresh chopped mint

225 g (8 oz/1¼ cups)
   cooked butterbeans
15 ml (1 tbsp) lemon juice
black pepper

1 Drain the tuna, reserving the water, and place in the food processor with the remaining ingredients.
2 Process until smooth, adding a little of the tuna water if necessary to make a soft pâté. If you do not have a processor, mash the ingredients together in a bowl with a fork.

HUMOUS AND CRUDITÉS (SERVES 4–6)

Humous can be used as a pâté, a sandwich spread, a filling for baked potatoes or served with a selection of vegetable crudités as a dip. Crudités could include: sticks of carrot, celery, pepper and courgette (zucchini); broccoli and cauliflower florets and whole cherry tomatoes.

I cheat if I am in a hurry and use tinned chickpeas.

225 g (8 oz/1¼ cups) cooked chickpeas
30 ml (2 tbsp) lemon juice
1 clove garlic (optional)
black pepper

60 ml (3 rounded tbsp) tahini paste
15 ml (1 tbsp) olive oil
2 spring onions (scallions)
a little water (if necessary)

1 Process all the ingredients until a soft, smooth pâté is obtained, using a little water if necessary.

AVOCADO AND TOMATO STARTER (SERVES 4)

1 large avocado
½ lettuce
60 ml (4 tbsp) French dressing (see Chapter 8, page 143)

1 large beef tomato
80 ml (4 tbsp) sprouted seeds e.g. lentils, mung beans, aduki beans

1 Peel, halve and stone the avocado. Halve the tomato.
2 Lay both the tomato and the avocado halves cut side down and cut each half into 6 wedges.
3 On serving plates, arrange beds of shredded lettuce. On top, arrange alternate slices of avocado and tomato to form an upturned boat shape.
4 Sprinkle with sprouted seeds, and serve with French dressing.

AVOCADO AND MANGO STARTER (SERVES 4)

Substitute mango for the tomato in the previous recipe. Arrange the avocado and mango in a fan shape. For special occasions, use the egg and prawn stuffing mixture from the Stuffed Lettuce Leaves recipe *(see page 58)* and pile at the point of each fan. Pour over the French dressing and, for those who can eat bread, use it to mop up the juices. Delicious!

COUNTRY SALAD (SERVES 4–6)

This salad is delicious just as it is, but you can add cubes of creamy goat's cheese and serve with crusty bread, if you are allowed such luxuries.

455 g (1 lb/3½ cups) waxy
   new potatoes
bunch asparagus or green beans
½ red pepper, sliced
1 courgette (zucchini), thinly sliced
15 ml (1 tbsp) fresh parsley
French dressing
   (see Chapter 8, page 143)

3 eggs, hardboiled
1 large avocado
½ yellow pepper, sliced
12 black olives (optional))
4 spring onions (scallions)
   finely sliced
black pepper

1 Cook the potatoes whole and in their skins until tender. Cool. Peel off the skins if preferred. Cut into large chunks.
2 Shell and quarter the hardboiled eggs.
3 Steam the asparagus or beans for no longer than 5 minutes. Cool and slice into 3-cm (1-in) lengths.
4 Peel and stone the avocado and cut the flesh into chunks.
5 Gently layer the ingredients in a serving bowl so that they look mixed but have not been broken by the tossing.
6 Pour the French dressing over just before serving, or serve separately.

SAVOURY FRUIT SALAD (SERVES 4–6)

Other vegetables and fruit could be substituted in this recipe.

1 avocado	15 ml (1 tbsp) lemon juice
30 ml (2 tbsp) olive oil	black pepper
½ melon, cubed	½ cucumber, peeled and diced
2 tomatoes, skinned and diced	10 ml (1 dsp) chopped mint

1 Skin and stone the avocado and cut the flesh into cubes.
2 Mix together the lemon juice, olive oil and black pepper.
3 Place all the ingredients in a bowl and combine very gently.
4 If possible, chill for a few hours to allow the flavours to mingle.

ASPARAGUS OR LEEKS WITH WALNUT MAYONNAISE (SERVES 4)

This is a delicious and unusual starter. Use a serrated knife for cutting the leeks; although not tough, they can be difficult to cut. The mayonnaise can be made by substituting 30 ml (2 tbsp) walnut oil for the other oils in the recipe.

1 bunch asparagus or	120 ml (8 tbsp) mayonnaise
4 long thin young leeks	(see Chapter 8, page 144)
15 g (½ oz/⅛ cup) walnuts,	
finely chopped	

1 If using the leeks, cut off and discard any green section. Halve each stem.
2 If using the asparagus, cut off the woody base of each stem.
3 Steam the leeks or asparagus for 5 minutes or until barely cooked. Cool quickly in cold water then drain.
4 Place the mayonnaise in a bowl and mix in most of the walnuts, reserving a few for garnishing.
5 Divide the leeks or asparagus between four plates and spoon the mayonnaise over the centre of each portion.
6 Garnish with the chopped walnuts.

HORS D'ŒUVRES WITH GARLIC MAYONNAISE (SERVES 4–6)

mayonnaise
  (see Chapter 8, page 144)

2 cloves garlic
55 g (2 oz/²/₃ cup) ground
  almonds

Serve with a selection of the following:

hardboiled eggs
tuna fish
sardines
baby sweetcorn
sugar snap peas
cooked broccoli

cherry tomatoes
whole radish
black olives
grilled peppers
cooked green beans

1 Make the mayonnaise using half olive oil and half a lighter oil, such as sunflower.
2 Press the garlic cloves and add to the mayonnaise with the ground almonds. Mix well.
3 Serve to accompany a selection of the hors d'œuvres.

Soups

Making soup is easy, as long as you have a good stock available. Instructions for making stock are given in the introduction *(see page 38)*. I always try to keep a supply of stock in the freezer, but do not be put off trying these recipes if you do not have ready-made stock as many are fine made with water. Those able to tolerate miso, shoyu/tamari sauce can use these to add extra flavour. However, avoid stock cubes in any form – I feel that the hydrolysed vegetable or meat protein which they contain is quite harmful.

A pan of soup is a useful standby. Served with a little rice, it makes an ideal mid-morning, afternoon or evening snack, and it can be used as a starter for lunch or evening meals.

Do not overcook soups. Beans and pulses obviously need cooking well but vegetables can be added at a later point and retain a better flavour and more vitamins if not overcooked. I rarely cook soups (except the beans) in a pressure cooker as it makes it too easy to overcook them.

Try cutting vegetables into different shapes to produce different-looking soups. For example, carrots can be finely diced, cut into matchstick pieces, sliced, grated, finely chopped in a food processor or left in rough chunks. Children will often eat soup more readily when it has been liquidized.

PEA SOUP (SERVES 4)

Split peas could be used if a quicker version of this soup is required but I feel the whole peas give a nicer flavour. Soak the split peas for 2 hours and cook for approximately 45 minutes.

170 g (6 oz/1 cup) dried whole peas
1–2 sticks (stalks) celery
1 large onion
30 ml (2 tbsp) fresh parsley
   or 5 ml (1 tsp) dried

1 litre (2 pints/5 cups) water or
   stock
3 ml (½ tsp) dried sage
2 ml (¼ tsp) dried thyme
black pepper

1 Soak the peas overnight in plenty of water.
2 Drain and rinse the peas. Cover with the stock or water, bring to the boil and simmer gently, covered with a lid, until soft and mushy. This will take approximately 1–1½ hours but only 10 minutes if using a pressure cooker. If not using a pressure cooker, you may need to add a little more water if the stock is evaporating.
3 Finely chop the celery and onion and add to the soup along with the dried sage, thyme, pepper and parsley. If using fresh parsley, add just before serving.
4 Bring to the boil and cook the soup for a further 15 minutes. Blend if a smoother soup is desired.

LIGHT LENTIL SOUP (SERVES 4)

This is a soup I make when I am in a hurry as it is so quick and easy. It tastes fine even without stock.

115 g (4 oz/½ cup) red split lentils
1 clove garlic
850 ml (1½ pints/3¾ cups)
   stock or water
5 ml (1 tsp) ground cumin
1 bay leaf

1 large onion
1 tin (400 g/15 oz/2 cups)
   chopped tomatoes
5 ml (1 tsp) grated lemon rind
2 ml (¼ tsp) ground cloves
black pepper

1 Wash the lentils, finely chop the onion and press the garlic.
2 Place all the ingredients into a saucepan, bring to the boil and simmer for 20–30 minutes.
3 Remove the bay leaf and serve.

FENNEL, CELERY AND LEEK SOUP (SERVES 4)

Extra celery and leeks can be used if you do not have any fennel. Omit the sweating stage if you prefer not to fry or if time is short.

2 medium leeks	3–4 sticks (stalks) celery
1 large bulb fennel	10 ml (1 dsp) olive oil
5 ml (1 tsp) fennel seeds	5 ml (1 tsp) celery seeds
570 ml (1 pint/2½ cups) water	425 ml (15 fl oz/2 cups) stock
285 ml (10 fl oz/1 ⅓ cups) soya or almond milk	black pepper

1 Finely slice the leeks and celery and dice the fennel.
2 Heat the oil in a pan and add the vegetables plus the fennel and celery seeds. Sweat, stirring occasionally, until the vegetables are softened and beginning to brown.
3 Add the water, bring to the boil and simmer for 10 minutes.
4 Allow to cool a little then process until smooth. This stage can be omitted if you prefer a chunky soup or you do not have a food processor. Return the mixture to the pan.
5 Add the remaining ingredients and bring to the boil.

LEEKIE MILLET BROTH (SERVES 4)

2 large leeks	2 large carrots
570 ml (1 pint/2½ cups) stock	570 ml (1 pint/2½ cups) water
3 ml (½ tsp) dried thyme	3 ml (½ tsp) dried rosemary
140 ml (5 fl oz/⅔ cup) soya or almond milk	45 g (1½ oz/½ cup) millet flakes
	black pepper

1 Slice the leeks and roughly chop the carrots.
2 Bring the stock and water to the boil and add the leeks, carrots, herbs and seasoning.
3 Bring to the boil again and simmer for 15 minutes.
4 Mix the millet flakes with the milk and stir into the soup. Bring to the boil, stirring until thickened, and simmer gently for 5 minutes before serving.

CARROT AND CORIANDER SOUP (SERVES 4)

If you do not have a food processor, or prefer your soup chunky, then grate the carrots and potato. Sweating can be omitted if desired.

455 g (1 lb/3¼ cups) carrots	1 large potato
1 large onion	10 ml (1 dsp) olive oil
850 ml (1½ pints/3¾ cups) stock	black pepper
45 ml (3 tbsp) fresh or frozen coriander	

1 Slice the carrots and dice the potato and onion.
2 Sweat the onion and potato in the oil until they begin to soften and brown.
3 Add the carrots, the stock and the pepper. Bring to the boil and simmer for 10–15 minutes.
4 Process the soup, return to the pan, add the coriander, heat through and serve.

CARROT AND CARDAMOM SOUP (SERVES 4)

Substitute 55 g (2 oz/¼ cup) red split lentils for the potato in the previous recipe and add 3 ml (½ tsp) ground cardamom instead of or as well as the fresh coriander. Add the lentils along with the carrots and cook for 15 minutes.

CARROT AND TOMATO SOUP (SERVES 4)

This is another soup I make if I'm in a hurry as it takes very little time to prepare and cook. If you do not have a food processor, finely grate the carrots and use ground almonds instead of the cashew nuts.

55 g (2 oz/½ cup) cashew nuts
3 medium carrots
570 ml (1 pt/2½ cups) stock or water
1 tin (400 g/15 oz/2 cups)
   chopped tomatoes in juice

3 ml (½ tsp) lemon rind
5 ml (1 tsp) mustard
15 ml (1 tbsp) chopped fresh
   coriander
black pepper

1 Process the cashew nuts until finely ground. Add the carrots and process again until the carrots are finely chopped.
2 Place all the ingredients in a pan, bring to the boil and simmer for 10 minutes before serving.

BUTTERBEAN AND VEGETABLE SOUP (SERVES 4)

225 g (8 oz/1 cup) butter beans
2 large carrots
1 large parsnip
2 ml (¼ tsp) dried thyme

1 litre (2 pints/5 cups) stock
   or water
2 leeks or onions
black pepper

1 Soak the butter beans overnight in lots of water.
2 Rinse the beans well and cook in the stock or water until soft, adding more water if the liquid is evaporating. To save time, use a pressure cooker if available and cook the beans for 10 minutes. The butter beans can be processed at this stage if a smoother soup is required.
3 Grate the carrots and parsnips and place in the pan with the beans.
4 Finely slice the leeks or onions and add to the pan along with the thyme and black pepper. Simmer for 15 minutes and serve.

QUICK VEGETABLE AND LENTIL SOUP (SERVES 4)

1 large onion	1 turnip
2 large carrots	3 sticks (stalks) celery
1 large leek	1 clove garlic
115 g (4 oz/½ cup) red split lentils	15 ml (1 tbsp) tomato
3 ml (½ tsp) dried sage	purée (optional)
2 ml (¼ tsp) dried marjoram	2 ml (¼ tsp) dried rosemary
2 ml (¼ tsp) dried oregano	3 ml (½ tsp) paprika
1½ litres (2½ pints/6 cups)	1 ml (⅛ tsp) cayenne pepper
stock or water	1 bay leaf

1 Cut all the vegetables into small pieces and press the garlic clove.
2 Place all the ingredients into a large pan, bring to the boil and simmer gently for 30 minutes. Remove the bay leaf.
3 Process if a smooth soup is required and serve.

PARSNIP AND ONION SOUP (SERVES 4)

If you do not wish to sweat, omit this stage. If you do not have a food processor, grate the parsnip and chop the onion very finely. For a creamier soup, add 140 ml (5 fl oz/⅔ cup) of soya or rice milk.

2 medium parsnips	1 large onion
10 ml (1 dsp) olive oil	3 ml (½ tsp) curry powder
3 ml (½ tsp) garam masala	black pepper
1 litre (2 pints/5 cups) stock	chopped walnuts to garnish

1 Dice the parsnips and onion and slowly sweat in the olive oil until they begin to brown, adding the spices and pepper for the last 2 minutes.
2 Add the stock and cook for 15 minutes.
3 Process the soup and serve with the walnuts floating on top.

FISH SOUP (SERVES 4)

This is a lovely way to eat fish and is ideal for serving to those a little wary of eating fish or to children.

2 medium onions	1 carrot
1 stick (stalk) celery	2 cloves garlic
1 tin (400 g/15 oz/2 cups) chopped tomatoes	1 litre (2 pints/5 cups) fish stock (see page 38)
juice of 1 orange	15 ml (1 tbsp) lemon juice
1 bay leaf	black pepper
455 g (1 lb/2¾ cups) cod or haddock	15 ml (1 tbsp) fresh parsley

1 Slice the onion, carrot and celery and press the garlic cloves.
2 Place all the ingredients except the fish and the parsley into a large pan. Bring to the boil and simmer for 10–15 minutes.
3 Cut or flake the fish into bite-sized pieces and add to the soup. Simmer for a further 5 minutes or until the fish is just cooked.
4 Serve sprinkled with parsley.

CAULIFLOWER AND CASHEW NUT SOUP (SERVES 4)

If you do not have a food processor, use ground almonds in place of the cashew nuts to thicken the soup.

1 onion	1 leek
10 ml (1 dsp) olive oil	1 small cauliflower
1 large parsnip	570 ml (20 fl oz/2½ cups) stock
55 g (2 oz/½ cup) cashew nuts	3 ml (½ tsp) curry powder
3 ml (½ tsp) mustard	2 ml (¼ tsp) thyme
black pepper	850 ml (1½ pints/3¾ cups) water

1 Chop the onion and leeks and sweat in the olive oil until they are soft.

2 Break the cauliflower into tiny florets, grate the parsnip and add to the pan along with the stock. Bring to the boil and then simmer for 10 minutes.
3 Process the cashew nuts until they are finely ground, then add half of the cauliflower mixture. Process again until smooth and creamy.
4 Return this mixture to the pan along with the remaining soup ingredients.
5 Bring to the boil and simmer for a further 5 minutes before serving.

GAZPACHO (SERVES 4)

455 g (1 lb/2¾ cups) fresh tomatoes
¼ small onion or
    4 spring onions (scallions)
20 ml (2 dsp) lemon juice
10 ml (1 dsp) fresh chopped parsley
extra parsley to garnish

1 small green pepper
½ large cucumber
black pepper
1 clove garlic (optional)
10 ml (1 dsp) fresh chopped mint

1 Skin the tomatoes by placing in boiling water for approximately 1 minute.
2 Roughly cut the vegetables, then process all the ingredients until a smooth mixture is obtained.
3 Serve chilled, garnished with parsley.

LEEK, SWEETCORN AND ALMOND SOUP (SERVES 4)

Use peas if you cannot tolerate corn. If you do not have a food processor, use ground almonds to thicken the soup.

1 large onion	680 g (1½ lb/6 cups) leeks
3 sticks (stalks) celery	10 ml (1 dsp) olive oil
85 g (3 oz/½ cup) whole almonds	850 ml (1½ pints/3¾ cups) water
570 ml (1 pint/2½ cups) stock	170 g (6 oz/1 cup) sweetcorn
3 ml (½ tsp) mustard (optional)	kernels
10 ml (1 dsp) fresh parsley	black pepper

1 Chop the onions, leeks and celery then sweat in the oil until the vegetables are soft and beginning to brown.
2 Process the almonds until finely ground, then add half the vegetable mixture and approximately 285 ml/½ pt/1⅓ cups of water. Process again until smooth and creamy.
3 Return this mixture to the pan along with the remaining ingredients.
4 Bring the soup to the boil and simmer for 10 minutes before serving.

MAJORCAN SOUP (SERVES 4)

This is my version of a soup I had while on holiday in Majorca. It looked disappointing when it arrived but it turned out to be delicious, despite its simple ingredients. It is a thick stew-type of soup but could be served watered down with more stock if desired.

2 onions	225 g (½ lb/4 cups) white cabbage
15 ml (1 tbsp) olive oil	black pepper
170 g (6 oz/1½ cups) mangetout	425 ml (15 fl oz/2 cups) good
or green beans	quality stock

1 Roughly chop the onions and cabbage and sweat them in the olive oil until they begin to soften and brown.

2 Add the beans or mangetout, the pepper and the stock, bring to the boil and simmer for 10 minutes before serving.

CHICKEN AND SEAWEED BROTH
(SERVES 4)

I make this soup whenever I have the remains of a chicken carcass, but it can be made without the chicken by substituting vegetable stock.

1 chicken carcass	1¾ litres (3 pints/7½ cups) water
2 onions	2 carrots
3 sticks (stalks) celery	10 ml (1 dsp) olive oil
2 strips wakame seaweed	10 ml (1 dsp) tomato purée
black pepper	(optional)

1 Cover the carcass with the water, bring to the boil and simmer for 45 minutes.
2 Remove any meat from the carcass and keep to one side. Discard the carcass.
3 Sieve the stock and preferably leave to stand overnight in the fridge to allow any fat to come to the surface.
4 Remove any fat from the stock by laying kitchen paper on the surface and allowing it to soak up the fat.
5 Chop the onions, carrots and celery and sweat in the oil until they begin to soften and brown.
6 Cut the wakame seaweed into small pieces using kitchen scissors. Soak the seaweed in a little water to soften, if necessary. Add to the pan along with the tomato purée and the black pepper.
7 Simmer for 15 minutes before serving.

Salads

When you mention a salad to most people it conjures up images of lettuce, tomato and cucumber and pangs of hunger for the rest of the afternoon or evening.

Salads need not be so. There is such a wide variety of vegetables, fruit and nuts which can be used that they need never be boring. Neither do they need to be lacking in substance. I never serve the typical lettuce, tomato and cucumber salad except as a side salad to accompany a substantial meal. Serve instead a selection of salads as a main course so that people can help themselves and pile their plates high. Any leftovers can be used for lunch the next day. In winter, serve a warm soup as a starter and a baked potato or hot rice dish with the salads.

Salads are easy to make because the quantity of ingredients is not that important. If you do not have all the ingredients for the following recipes, substitute your favourite ingredients or whatever you have available. You can go on inventing new salads for ever.

Salads make ideal starters. If you want a two-course meal or feel you eat insufficient raw food then try serving some of the following salads as starters.

The following recipes all serve at least four adults and in many cases there will be some left over for lunch the next day.

A Variety of Salads

A delicious meal can be had by making lots of different salads out of whatever ingredients you have available. Do not worry about the quantities and use fresh fruit, dried fruit, nuts and seeds as well as vegetables and herbs. Dressings could include mayonnaise, soya yogurt and French dressing, where appropriate. Try to group ingredients so that colours, flavours and textures complement each other.

Below are suggestions and approximate quantities. The ingredients just need mixing. Omit the French dressing if desired.

TUNA AND BEAN SALAD

1 tin (200 g/15 oz/1 $\frac{1}{3}$ cups) tuna
diced flesh of 1 small orange
55 g (2 oz/$\frac{1}{2}$ cup) toasted cashew nuts

115 g (4 oz/$\frac{2}{3}$ cup) red kidney
beans
15 ml (1 tbsp) French dressing
(optional)

AVOCADO AND GRAPEFRUIT SALAD

diced flesh of 1 red grapefruit
5 ml (1 tsp) grated ginger

diced flesh of 1 ripe avocado
225 g (8 oz/4 cups) spinach
leaves, chopped

COURGETTE (ZUCCHINI) AND CAULIFLOWER SALAD

2 courgettes (zucchini), sliced
5 ml (1 tsp) caraway seeds,
mayonnaise or French dressing

$\frac{1}{2}$ small cauliflower, broken into
small florets

BEANSPROUT AND SWEETCORN SALAD

55 g (2 oz/$\frac{2}{3}$ cup) beansprouts
$\frac{1}{2}$ diced cucumber
2 tomatoes, skinned and diced

115 g (4 oz/1 cup) sweetcorn
kernels

ROOT VEGETABLE AND RAISIN SALAD

1 grated turnip, celeriac or kohlrabi
30 ml (2 tbsp) raisins

1 large grated carrot
30 ml (2 tbsp) French dressing
or orange juice

APPLE, CELERY AND BEETROOT SALAD

1 large cooked beetroot, cubed
1 eating apple, sliced (leave the skin on)
15 ml (1 tbsp) French dressing
1 stick (stalk) celery, diced
15 ml (1 tbsp) chopped walnuts

BEAN AND PEPPER SALAD

225 g (8 oz/1¼ cups) mixed beans
½ red pepper, diced
15 ml (1 tbsp) fresh herbs
2 chopped spring onions
   (scallions)
15 ml (1 tbsp) French dressing

BEAN AND SWEETCORN SALAD

225 g (8 oz/1¼ cups) red kidney beans
225 g (8 oz/1¼ cups) sweetcorn
   kernels
170 g (6 oz/2 cups) cooked green
   beans (cut into 2.5-cm/
   1-in lengths)

CARROT AND BEETROOT SALAD

225 g (8 oz/1 ⅓ cups) grated
   raw carrot
2 sticks (stalks) celery, diced
30 ml (2 tbsp) French dressing
225 g (8 oz/1 ⅓ cups) grated raw
   beetroot
30 ml (2 tbsp) sultanas (optional)

AVOCADO, SMOKED TOFU
AND PINEAPPLE SALAD

diced flesh of 1 large avocado
1 cup chopped pineapple
170 g (6 oz/1 cup) diced
   smoked tofu

BEETROOT AND PINEAPPLE SALAD

5 medium beetroot, diced
30 ml (2 tbsp) chopped walnuts
1 cup chopped pineapple
8 pitted prunes, chopped
   (optional)
10 ml (1 dsp) lemon juice

RICE, SWEETCORN AND BEAN SALAD

115 g (4 oz/^{2}/$_3$ cup) cooked brown rice
55 g (2 oz/^{1}/$_3$ cup) red kidney beans
15 ml (1 tbsp) fresh herbs
   (mint, parsley, chives etc.)
55 g (2 oz/^{1}/$_3$ cup) sweetcorn or
   peas
15 ml (1 tbsp) French dressing

RICE AND CARROT SALAD

115 g (4 oz/^{2}/$_3$ cup) cooked brown rice
1 stick (stalk) celery, diced
2 spring onions (scallions), sliced
15 ml (1 tbsp) fresh herbs
15 ml (1 tbsp) French dressing
1 grated carrot
3 radishes, sliced
30 ml (2 tbsp) toasted sunflower
   seeds

HAZELNUT AND RICE SALAD

170 g (6 oz/1 cup) cooked brown rice
3 ml (^{1}/$_2$ tsp) ground cinnamon
30 ml (2 tbsp) toasted sesame seeds
6 chopped dried apricots (optional)
30 ml (2 tbsp) French dressing
30 ml (2 tbsp) raisins (optional)
30 ml (2 tbsp) toasted, chopped
   hazelnuts
5 ml (1 tsp) grated ginger

LEAF GREENS, ARAME AND SATSUMA SALAD

chopped greens (lettuce, spinach,
   Chinese leaves, watercress)
2 satsumas, segmented
30 g (1 oz/^{1}/$_2$ cup) arame seaweed
   soaked in water until soft
French dressing

BROCCOLI AND RED BEAN SALAD

340 g (12 oz/6 cups) broccoli florets
2 sticks (stalks) celery, sliced
2 spring onions (scallions), sliced
115 g (4 oz/^{1}/$_2$ cup) red kidney
   beans
French dressing

PINEAPPLE AND OLIVE SALAD

salad greens (Chinese leaves, spinach, cress)
12 black olives

½ cup pineapple pieces
2 tomatoes, cut into segments
5-cm (2-in) piece cucumber, cubed

AVOCADO, SWEETCORN AND OLIVE SALAD

1 avocado, diced
12 black olives, halved

½ cup sweetcorn or peas
15 ml (1 tbsp) French dressing

The following salads also make excellent accompaniments to curries.

CUCUMBER, MINT AND YOGURT SALAD

½ cucumber, peeled and diced
15 ml (1 tbsp) chopped mint

2.5-cm (1-in) piece ginger, grated
140 ml (5 fl oz/⅔ cup) soya yogurt

TOMATO AND CORIANDER SALAD

5 large tomatoes, skinned and sliced
2 spring onions (scallions), finely sliced
French dressing

15 ml (1 tbsp) chopped fresh coriander

APPLE, CARROT AND GINGER SALAD

1 grated apple
10 ml (1 dsp) grated ginger

1 large grated carrot
15 ml (1 tbsp) French dressing

ALL IN ONE SALAD

One of my favourite meals is a bowl of salad which contains any-thing I have available. Serve this on its own, with baked potatoes, boiled new potatoes or with a savoury rice salad.

In a large bowl put *any* of the following ingredients in *any* quantities until you have sufficient salad. Mix gently and serve, dressed if you like with French dressing:

- shredded lettuce, spinach, Chinese leaves, white cabbage or red cabbage
- grated carrot, parsnip, celeriac or kohlrabi
- diced cucumber, avocado, pepper, tomato, fennel, peach or apple
- sliced celery, radish, spring onion (scallion) or courgette (zucchini)
- florets of cauliflower and broccoli
- sweetcorn kernels, fresh peas, broad beans, olives or grapes
- cooked beans e.g. chickpeas or red kidney beans
- chopped, flaked or toasted nuts and seeds
- fresh herbs e.g. mint, chives, parsley
- watercress, mustard cress, sprouted seeds.

COLESLAW

An alternative coleslaw can be made by adding 80 ml (4 rounded tbsp) mayonnaise instead of the dressing.

225 g (8 oz/4 cups) white cabbage
1 small eating apple
1 large carrot
20 ml (1 tbsp) sultanas

½ bulb fennel or
   2 sticks (stalks) celery
40 ml (2 tbsp) chopped walnuts

Dressing
45 ml (3 tbsp) olive oil
3 ml (½ tsp) mustard
1 spring onion (scallion), finely sliced

15 ml (1 tbsp) lemon juice
3 ml (½ tsp) grated ginger

1 Shred the cabbage and fennel finely. Chop the celery and the unpeeled apple. Grate the carrot.
2 Shake the dressing ingredients together in a screw-topped jar.
3 Mix all the coleslaw ingredients and the dressing together in a bowl.

CURRIED APPLE COLESLAW

If preferred, a French dressing could be used instead of the mayonnaise and yogurt.

225 g (8 oz/4 cups) white cabbage
2 large sticks (stalks) celery
1 red eating apple

8 radishes
2 spring onions (scallions)
10 ml (2 tsp) caraway seeds

Dressing
60 ml (3 rounded tbsp) mayonnaise
60 ml (3 rounded tbsp) soya yogurt or extra mayonnaise
10 ml (1 dsp) lemon juice
3 ml (½ tsp) curry powder

1 Shred the cabbage. Slice the radishes, the celery, the spring onions (scallions) and the unpeeled apple.
2 Mix the dressing ingredients together.
3 Combine all the ingredients in a large bowl.

MINTED AVOCADO AND CHICKPEA SALAD

This salad makes a lovely starter served on a bed of crisp lettuce.

115 g (4 oz/½ cup) chickpeas
1 large banana
1 medium ripe avocado
15 ml (1 tbsp) lemon juice

60 ml (3 rounded tbsp mayonnaise)
5 ml (1 tsp) fresh mint
1 clove garlic, optional
paprika to garnish

1 Cook the chickpeas until tender and allow to cool.
2 Slice the banana and dice the avocado flesh into a bowl. Toss gently in the lemon juice.
3 Stir in the remaining ingredients and garnish with paprika.

CHICKEN, EGG, ALMOND AND POTATO SALAD

Avocado can be used if you cannot tolerate eggs, and cooked butter beans can be substituted for the chicken.

225 g (8 oz/2 cups) new potatoes
2 hardboiled eggs
55 g (2 oz/½ cup) toasted flaked almonds

115 g (4 oz/1 cup) cooked chicken
80 ml (4 rounded tbsp) mayonnaise

1 Cook the potatoes in their skins and, when cool, skin and dice.
2 Roughly chop the chicken and hardboiled eggs.
3 Mix all the ingredients together.

TUNA AND CELERY SALAD

2 sticks (stalks) celery
1 tin (200 g/7 oz/1⅓ cups)
   tuna in water

225 g (8 oz/1⅓ cups) cooked rice
mayonnaise, soya yogurt or
   French dressing

1 Cut and finely dice the celery and combine with the rice and drained tuna.
2 Use sufficient French dressing, mayonnaise or yogurt to bind the ingredients. I like to use a mixture of yogurt and mayonnaise.

JELLIED BEETROOT SALAD

Gelozone is the vegetarian alternative to gelatine.

285 ml (½ pint/1 ⅓ cups) orange juice
340 g (12 oz/2 cups) cooked beetroot

3 g (1 level tsp) Gelozone

1 Pour the fruit juice into a pan and sprinkle the Gelozone on top. Stir until dissolved. Bring the mixture to the boil, stirring all the time.
2 Cube the beetroot and add to the pan. Mix.
3 Pour into a serving dish and refrigerate until set and cold.

JELLIED CARROT SALAD

Follow the previous recipe but add 225 g (8 oz/1 $^1/_3$ cups) finely grated raw carrot instead of the beetroot. Try other flavoured fruit juices.

MILLET TABOULI

Tabouli is traditionally made with couscous which is made from wheat. Use this, if you are allowed, as it is delicious. Just add the uncooked couscous to the salad instead of the millet. It will soften by soaking up the juices. Allow to stand for 2 hours before serving.

85 g (3 oz/½ cup) whole millet
¼ red pepper
1 stick (stalk) celery
15 ml (1 tbsp) chopped parsley
10 ml (1 dsp) chopped chives
   or spring onions (scallions)

4 large tomatoes
¼ cucumber
30 ml (2 tbsp) fresh chopped mint
   (essential)
30 ml (2 tbsp) French dressing

1 Cook the millet in 425 ml (¾ pint/2 cups) of boiling water for 10–15 minutes. Sieve the millet and allow to cool.
2 Skin and finely chop the tomatoes. Finely dice the pepper, cucumber and celery.
3 Mix the millet, salad vegetables, herbs and French dressing together and leave to stand for a few hours to allow the flavours to mingle.

MEDITERRANEAN LENTIL SALAD

170 g (6 oz/1 cup) whole lentils
1 clove garlic
15 ml (1 tbsp) lemon juice
3 ml (½ tsp) orange rind
2 spring onions (scallions)
¼ green pepper
40 ml (2 tbsp) currants, optional

1 orange
30 ml (2 tbsp) olive oil
3 ml (½ tsp) lemon rind
1 small carrot
¼ red pepper
5 ml (1 tsp) fresh parsley, chives
   and mint

1 Cook the lentils for approximately 15–20 minutes in lots of water until soft but not mushy. Drain.
2 Chop the orange flesh and press the garlic clove.
3 Add to the lentils along with the oil, lemon juice and the orange and lemon rind whilst the lentils are still warm. Allow to cool.
4 Grate the carrot, dice the peppers, slice the spring onions (scallions) and finely chop the herbs.
5 When cool, combine all the salad ingredients and, if possible, stand for 1 hour before serving to allow the flavours to mix.

RICE PILAF RING

Serve as it is or fill the centre with Tropical Curried Chicken Salad *(page 88)* or Minted Avocado and Chickpea Salad *(page 83)*. The French dressing can be omitted – the pilaf should still stick together provided the rice has been cooked sufficiently.

1 large onion	15 ml (1 tbsp) olive oil
225 g (8 oz/1 cup) brown rice	45 g (1½ oz/¼ cup) dried apricots
55 g (2 oz/½ cup) walnuts	45 g (1½ oz/¼ cup) raisins
570 ml (1 pint/2½ cups) water	1 bay leaf
3 ml (½ tsp) cinnamon	black pepper
30 ml (2 tbsp) French dressing	

1 Dice the onion and sweat in the oil for approximately 10 minutes.
2 Soak the rice in cold water for 15 minutes. Rinse and drain.
3 Finely chop the apricots and walnuts and add to the pan with the rice, the raisins, the water and the spices.
4 Bring to the boil, cover and simmer for approximately 40 minutes until the rice is cooked and all the water has been absorbed. If necessary, add a little more water during cooking.
5 Remove the bay leaf and stir in the French dressing while still warm. Press into a ring mould and leave to cool.

RED CABBAGE SALAD

This dish can be served hot as a vegetable or allowed to cool and served as a salad. It can be cooked on the top of the stove, but be careful as it will quickly dry out and burn.

455 g (1 lb/8 cups) red cabbage
1 large baking apple
60 ml (2 fl oz/¼ cup) water
10 ml (1 dsp) lemon juice
3 ml (½ tsp) lemon rind

1 onion
40 ml (2 tbsp) raisins, optional
juice of 1 orange
3 ml (½ tsp) orange rind

1 Chop the red cabbage, slice the onion and grate the apple.
2 Mix all the ingredients together in a casserole dish. Cover and cook in the oven at 400°F/200°C/gas mark 6 for approximately 1 hour, stirring once during cooking.

CURRIED EGG AND RICE SALAD

Avocado can be substituted for the hardboiled eggs.

170 g (6 oz/¾ cup) brown rice
5 ml (1 tsp) curry powder
10 ml (1 dsp) tomato purée
60 ml (3 rounded tbsp) mayonnaise

1 medium onion
5 ml (1 tsp) paprika
4 hardboiled eggs
60 ml (3 tbsp) soya yogurt or
    extra mayonnaise

1 Cook the rice and allow to cool.
2 Finely dice the onion and cook in 30 ml (2 tbsp) water for 5 minutes.
3 Stir the curry powder, paprika and tomato purée into the onions and allow to cool.
4 Coarsely chop the hardboiled eggs, then stir all the ingredients gently together.

TROPICAL CURRIED CHICKEN SALAD

This makes a delicious filling for the Rice Pilaf Ring *(page 86)* or it can be served as one of a selection of salads or as a starter on a bed of lettuce garnished with toasted coconut. Vegetarians could substitute butter beans for the chicken.

2 bananas
340 g (12 oz/2½ cups) cooked chicken
55 g (2 oz/⅓ cup) toasted cashews

15 ml (1 tbsp) lemon juice
55 g (2 oz/¼ cup) dried apricots
30 g (1 oz/⅙ cup) sultanas, optional

Dressing
2 spring onions
3 ml (½ tsp) curry powder
80 ml (4 rounded tbsp) mayonnaise

¼ eating apple
3 ml (½ tsp) lemon juice

1 To make the dressing, slice the spring onions and finely grate the apple before combining the dressing ingredients.
2 Slice the bananas and toss in the lemon juice to prevent browning.
3 Cut the chicken into bite-sized chunks and dice the apricots into small pieces.
4 Place all the ingredients together and gently mix with the dressing.

VEGETABLE CHILLI WITH WALNUTS AND QUINOA (SERVES 4)

If you do not have a food processor, use ground almonds instead of ground walnuts. Millet could be used instead of the quinoa, and other favourite vegetables substituted. If you prefer not to fry, miss out the sweating stage.

115 g (4 oz/^{2}/$_3$ cup) quinoa
1 carrot
15 ml (1 tbsp) olive oil
½ red pepper
225 g (8 oz/1 ⅓ cups) cooked
 red kidney beans
juice and rind of 1 orange
10 ml (1 dsp) paprika

1 onion
2 sticks (stalks) celery
2 courgettes (zucchini)
115 g (4 oz/1 cup) walnut halves
570 ml (1 pt/2½ cups) carrot
 or tomato juice
3 ml (½ tsp) nutmeg
black pepper

1 Cook the quinoa in 425 ml (¾ pint/2 cups) boiling water for 15 minutes.
2 Dice the onion, carrot and celery, and sweat in the oil until they begin to soften and brown.
3 Finely dice the courgettes (zucchini) and the red pepper. Add to the pan along with the other vegetables, and continue to sweat until they are beginning to soften.
4 Process two-thirds of the walnuts until they are finely ground, and add these to the vegetables along with the remaining walnuts broken into smaller pieces and the quinoa mixture.
5 Add the remaining ingredients, mix well and spoon into a large, shallow gratin dish. Bake uncovered in the centre of the oven at 400°F/200°C/gas mark 6 for 30 minutes.

LENTIL BOLOGNESE (SERVES 4)

Serve with rice or pasta, as a filling for baked potatoes, as a stuffing for vegetables, taco shells or in a lasagne. I always make up double the quantity of this recipe as it freezes well and is a super standby. If tomatoes are not tolerated, use carrot juice.

115 g (4 oz/²/₃ cup) brown lentils
½ green pepper
1 carrot
285 ml (½ pt/1 ⅓ cups) water
5 ml (1 tsp) dried oregano
5 ml (1 tsp) dried basil
black pepper

1 onion
1 stick (stalk) celery
2 cloves garlic
570 ml (1 pt/2½ cups) creamed
  tomatoes or tomato juice
1 bay leaf

1 Wash the lentils well.
2 Finely chop the onion, green pepper and celery. Dice the carrot and press the garlic cloves.
3 Place all the ingredients into a pan, bring to the boil and simmer, covered, for 30 minutes or until the lentils are soft but not mushy.

LENTIL MOUSSAKA (SERVES 4)

1 portion Lentil Bolognese
  (see above)
1 aubergine (eggplant)

3 courgettes (zucchini)
680 g (1½ lb/5 cups) potatoes
10 ml (1 dsp) olive oil

1 Place half the lentil mix into a large, shallow ovenproof dish.
2 Cut the courgettes (zucchini) and aubergine (eggplant) into 1½-cm (½-in) slices and place in layers on top of the lentils. Cover with the remaining lentil mix.
3 Peel the potatoes and cut into ¼-cm (⅛-in) slices, using a food processor if available. Layer these on top of the lentils and vegetables.
4 Brush the top with olive oil and bake at 400°F/200°C/gas mark 6 for 1¼ hours until the potatoes are cooked and crisp.

VEGETARIAN SHEPHERDS PIE (SERVES 4)

An alternative topping could be made by mixing cooked millet and mashed parsnips in roughly equal quantities.

680 g (1½ lb/5 cups) potatoes
10 ml (1 dsp) olive oil

1 portion Lentil Bolognese
(see page 90)

1 Cook the potatoes until soft and mash with a small amount of the cooking liquid until fluffy.
2 Place the Lentil Bolognese into a shallow ovenproof dish.
3 Spread the potatoes on top, level the surface and brush with olive oil.
4 Bake for 45 minutes at 400°F/200°C/gas mark 6. Place under the grill for a few minutes if the surface has not browned sufficiently.

CARROT AND COURGETTE (ZUCCHINI) BAKE (SERVES 4)

Serve with baked potatoes and a selection of salads.

1 onion, diced
2 courgettes (zucchini), grated
2 eggs
30 g (1 oz/¹/₆ cup) rice flour
3 ml (½ tsp) potassium baking powder
3 ml (½ tsp) dried rosemary
black pepper

10 ml (1 dsp) olive oil
2 carrots, grated
55 g (2 oz/¹/₃ cup) maize meal
115 ml (4 fl oz/½ cup) soya or
almond milk
3 ml (½ tsp) dried thyme

1 Sweat the onion in the oil until it begins to soften and brown.
2 Mix in a bowl the onion, courgettes (zucchini) and carrots.
3 Beat the eggs with the maize meal, rice flour, milk, baking powder, herbs and black pepper. Combine the two mixtures.
4 Pour into a greased gratin dish and bake uncovered at 400°F/200°C/gas mark 6 for 45 minutes to 1 hour or until brown and set.

MILLET AND WALNUT BAKE (SERVES 4)

Serve hot with salads, vegetables or baked potatoes.

Omit the sweating if you prefer. Other vegetables can be substituted for a variation.

The original recipe for this dish uses couscous instead of millet. If you are allowed wheat, try it, as it really does make a delicious bake. Just add 85 g (3 oz/½ cup) of couscous along with the remaining ingredients, and add a total of 850 ml (1½ pints/3¾ cups) of liquid, including the vegetable juice. The couscous will soak up the liquid as it cooks. A little grated cheese on top of this will make even the most ardent meat-eaters start thinking vegetarian.

570 ml (1 pt/2½ cups) tomato, carrot or vegetable juice
1 onion
1 carrot
115 g (4 oz/1 cup) walnuts
3 ml (½ tsp) dried thyme
black pepper

570 ml (1 pt/2½ cups) water
115 g (4 oz/²/₃ cup) millet grain
1 large stick (stalk) celery
2 medium courgettes (zucchini)
15 ml (1 tbsp) olive oil
3 ml (½ tsp) dried rosemary

1 Mix the vegetable juice and the water and cook the millet for 20 minutes in 570 ml (1 pint/2½ cups) of this liquid.
2 Finely chop the onion and celery, finely dice the carrot and courgettes (zucchini). Process the walnuts in a food processor until they are roughly ground.
3 Sweat the onion, carrot and celery in the oil until they start to soften and brown. Add the courgettes (zucchini) and sweat for a few more minutes.
4 Add the millet mixture, the remaining liquid, the nuts, herbs and pepper.
5 Mix well and place in a large, shallow, ovenproof dish.
6 Bake uncovered in the centre of the oven for 30 minutes at 400°F/200°C/gas mark 6.

CAULIFLOWER AND COURGETTE BAKE
(SERVES 4)

Serve hot with potatoes or rice and salads or vegetables.

680 g (1½ lb/6 cups) cauliflower, divided into florets
5 ml (1 tsp) mustard
3 eggs, separated
10 ml (1 dsp) olive oil

2 courgettes (zucchini)
45 ml (3 tbsp) rice flour
140 ml (5 fl oz/⅔ cup) soya or almond milk

1 Cook the cauliflower for approximately 5 minutes in boiling water until just tender.
2 Cut the courgettes (zucchini) into 1-cm (¼-in) slices.
3 Mix the flour and mustard with the milk in a pan and bring gently to the boil, stirring all the time. Simmer for 1 minute. The sauce will be very thick.
4 Blend the cauliflower, egg yolks and white sauce in a food processor until smooth.
5 Whisk the egg whites until stiff and fold into the cauliflower mixture with a large metal spoon.
6 Spoon half the mixture into a greased gratin dish. Arrange half the courgettes (zucchini) on top, then cover with the remaining cauliflower mixture. Top with the remaining courgette (zucchini) and brush with olive oil.
7 Bake at 400°F/200°C/gas mark 6 for approximately 30 minutes or until golden brown and set.

SAVOURY PANCAKES (SERVES 4)

Stuffed pancakes take a little time to prepare but are worth the effort for special meals. Even confirmed meat-eaters will love them. To save time, pancakes can be made in bulk and frozen.

1 egg
5 ml (1 level tsp) potassium
   baking powder
10 ml (1 dsp) olive oil

115 g (4 oz/^{2}/$_3$ cup) rice flour
60 ml (2 fl oz/^{1}/$_4$ cup) water
170 ml (6 fl oz/^{3}/$_4$ cup) soya milk

1 Blend all the ingredients except the oil in the food processor. If mixing by hand, beat the egg then add the remaining ingredients except the oil and beat well.
2 Oil a griddle or frying pan and cook 4 pancakes. Turn as soon as the pancakes are puffed and full of bubbles.

RATATOUILLE-STUFFED PANCAKES

Fill four pancakes with Ratatouille *(see Chapter 8, page 147)* and place in one large or four small gratin dishes. Cover with White Sauce *(see Chapter 8, page 145)* and sprinkle the surface with chopped nuts or, if allowed, a mixture of breadcrumbs and grated cheese. Place in a hot oven or under the grill to warm through and brown.

VEGETABLE MASALA PANCAKES

Follow the previous recipe but use the Vegetable Masala ingredients to stuff the pancakes with *(see page 118)*.

LENTIL BOLOGNESE PANCAKES

Follow the recipe on page 000, but use the Lentil Bolognese ingredients to stuff the pancakes with *(see page 90)*.

BLACK EYED BEAN AND VEGETABLE TERRINE (SERVES 4)

Serve hot or cold with a selection of vegetables or salads. Substitute cooked millet or quinoa for the rice if desired.

170 g (6 oz/1 cup) black eyed beans	1 large onion
2 sticks (stalks) celery	1 courgette (zucchini)
1 medium carrot	1 clove garlic
10 ml (1 dsp) olive oil	10 ml (1 dsp) fresh parsley
10 ml (1 dsp) fresh coriander	115 g (4 oz/^{2}/$_3$ cup) cooked rice
3 ml ($\frac{1}{2}$ tsp) grated lemon rind	black pepper
3 ml ($\frac{1}{2}$ tsp) dried basil	2ml ($\frac{1}{4}$ tsp) dried thyme
5 ml (1 tsp) grated ginger	

1 Soak the black eyed beans overnight. Rinse and then cook in lots of water until quite soft. Sieve to remove the cooking liquid.
2 Finely dice the onion, celery and courgette (zucchini), grate the carrot and press the garlic clove. Sweat the onion, celery and garlic in the oil until they begin to soften and brown. Add the courgette (zucchini) and carrot and continue cooking until they too begin to soften.
3 Finely chop the parsley and coriander and place in a bowl along with the rest of the ingredients. Mix together but do not be gentle as the beans should partially break up, making the mixture quite soft.
4 Place in a greased loaf tin and bake in the centre of the oven at 400°F/200°C/gas mark 6 for approximately 45 minutes or until the loaf is beginning to brown around the edges.

NUTTY VEGETABLE LOAF (SERVES 4)

Serve hot with vegetables, salads, rice or potatoes and with a sauce from Chapter 8, such as Fresh Tomato (see page 147), Onion (see page 145) or Vegetable Purée (see page 148). Alternatively, serve cold with a selection of salads. You can replace the tomato purée with 5 ml (1 tsp) miso, and the vegetables can also be varied.

1 onion	½ red pepper
10 ml (1 dsp) olive oil	1 medium carrot, grated
½ medium baking apple, grated	115 g (4 oz/²/₃ cup) cooked brown
55 g (2 oz/½ cup) nuts, finely ground,	rice, buckwheat or millet
e.g. hazelnuts, walnuts	10 ml (1 dsp) tomato purée
2 ml (¼ tsp) dried thyme	2 ml (¼ tsp) dried rosemary
2 ml (¼ tsp) nutmeg	1 ml (⅛ tsp) cayenne pepper
5 ml (1 tsp) mustard, optional	black pepper

1 Finely dice the onion and red pepper, and sweat in the oil until they soften and begin to brown.
2 Add the grated carrot and apple and sweat for another few minutes until they too begin to soften.
3 Combine all the ingredients and mix well.
4 Place the mixture in a greased loaf tin and bake covered for approximately 40 minutes in the centre of the oven at 400°F/200°C/gas mark 6.

SQUIRREL'S DELIGHT (SERVES 4)

Serve hot with vegetables, salads, rice or potatoes and with a sauce from Chapter 8, such as Fresh Tomato *(see page 147)*, Onion *(see page145)* or Vegetable Purée *(see page 148)*.

1 onion	1 stick (stalk) celery
55 g (2 oz/½ cup) mushrooms (optional)	1 clove garlic
10 ml (1 dsp) olive oil	55 g (2 oz/½ cup) chopped
85 g (3 oz/¾ cup) chopped cashews	almonds
30 g (1 oz/¹/₃ cup) ground almonds	2 eggs or an egg replacer
60 ml (3 tbsp) sweetcorn or peas	115 g (4 oz/²/₃ cup) cooked millet,
15 ml (1 tbsp) fresh chopped coriander	rice, quinoa or buckwheat
30 ml (2 tbsp) fresh chopped parsley	3 ml (½ tsp) grated lemon rind
10 ml (1 dsp) lemon juice	5 ml (1 level tsp) ground coriander
3 ml (½ level tsp) cinnamon	2 pinches ground cloves
2ml (¼ tsp) fennel seeds	black pepper

1 Finely dice the onion, celery and mushrooms and press the garlic clove.
2 Sweat the onion, garlic and celery in the oil until they soften and begin to brown. Add the mushrooms and sweat for 2 minutes.
3 Mix all the ingredients together.
4 Place in a greased loaf tin and cover with foil.
5 Bake at 400°F/200°C/gas mark 6 for approximately 45 minutes. For a more moist loaf steam over a pan of water for 45 minutes or pressure cook for 15 minutes.

NUT ROAST (SERVES 4)

This loaf remains moist because of the way it is cooked. It can be served hot and is delicious with the Orange and Ginger Sauce from the Vegetable and Fruit Kebab recipe *(see page 98)*. However, it can also be served cold with salads or as a pâté.

The original recipe contained 55 g (2 oz/1 cup) of breadcrumbs instead of the rice, so try this as a variation if you are allowed bread. If permitted, use 3 ml (½ tsp) miso to make a tasty stock.

1 small onion	2 large mushrooms or 1 stick
1 large tomato	(stalk) celery
10 ml (1 dsp) olive oil	10 ml (1 level dsp) rice flour
90 ml (3 fl oz/⅓ cup) water or stock	2ml (¼ tsp) dried rosemary
2ml (¼ tsp) dried thyme	30 g (1 oz/¼ cup) almonds
55 g (2 oz/½ cup) hazelnuts	30 g (1 oz/¼ cup) cashews
115 g (4 oz/⅔ cup) cooked rice,	1 egg (optional)
millet or quinoa	black pepper

1 Finely dice the onion, mushrooms (or celery), and skin and dice the tomato.
2 Sweat the onion in the oil until soft. Add the mushrooms or celery and cook for 2–3 minutes. Stir in the tomato, cover and simmer for 3 minutes.
3 Sprinkle on the flour and cook for 1 minute, stirring continuously. Gradually stir in the stock or water. Add the herbs and cook for 2 minutes.

4 Grind the nuts roughly and add along with the rice, egg and pepper.
5 Pack the mixture into a terrine or loaf tin, cover with foil and tuck the edges under to secure tightly.
6 Steam for 45 minutes above a pan of boiling water or pressure cook for 15 minutes.

VEGETABLE AND FRUIT KEBABS WITH ORANGE AND GINGER SAUCE (SERVES 4)

If fresh sweetcorn is not available, use frozen. Use a carton of orange juice rather than fresh oranges as this is not quite as acidic and makes the sauce less sharp. Another vegetable could be substituted for the mushrooms or sweetcorn, such as onion or tomatoes, and cubes of chicken or lamb could be used instead of the bananas. For extra flavour, add 30 ml (2 tbsp) of shoyu/tamari sauce (if allowed). This will also enable water to be used instead of the stock.

Kebabs

2 corn on the cob	2 large courgettes (zucchini)
1 red pepper	2 bananas
8 medium mushrooms	4 large or 8 small skewers

Sauce

140 ml (5 fl oz/^{2}/$_3$ cup) orange juice	5 ml (1 tsp) grated orange rind
5 ml (1 tsp) grated ginger	20 ml (2 dsp) sunflower oil
5 ml (1 tsp) mustard	pinch cayenne pepper
black pepper	2 cloves garlic
285 ml (10 fl oz/1 ^{1}/$_3$ cups) good stock	15 ml (1 level tbsp) cornflour (cornstarch)

1 Make a marinade by mixing all the sauce ingredients except the stock and cornflour (cornstarch).
2 Cut the sweetcorn, courgettes (zucchini), pepper and bananas into 8 pieces. Place all the vegetables and fruit into a Tupperware container with a tight-fitting lid. Pour over the marinade

and allow to stand for at least 2 hours, turning the container occasionally to coat the vegetables.

3 Thread the kebab ingredients onto 4 large or 8 small skewers.

4 Place the kebabs on a baking tray, cover with foil and bake in the oven at 400°F/200°C/gas mark 6 for 30 minutes.

5 Pour the remaining marinade into a pan together with the stock and the cornflour (cornstarch). Mix until smooth and bring the sauce to the boil, stirring constantly. When the kebabs have cooked, pour any juices from the tray into the sauce.

6 Place the kebabs on a bed of rice and serve with the sauce poured over. Accompany with a crisp salad.

VEGETABLE RISOTTO (SERVES 4)

For extra flavour, add 5 ml (1 tsp) finely sliced fresh ginger or, if acceptable, 15 ml (1 tbsp) shoyu/tamari sauce. To add interest, vary the vegetables (try green beans, mangetout, broccoli or cauliflower, for example), and use millet, buckwheat or quinoa instead of the rice. Try serving with Tomato Sauce *(see Chapter 8, page 147)*.

170 g (6 oz/¾ cup) brown rice	2 carrots
1 small parsnip	1 onion
1 stick (stalk) celery	1 courgette (zucchini)
10 ml (1 dsp) olive oil	handful beansprouts
40 ml (2 tbsp) sweetcorn or frozen peas	55 g (2 oz/½ cup) toasted
15 ml (1 tbsp) parsley	slivered almonds
black pepper	30 ml (2 tbsp) water

1 Boil the rice until just cooked. Sieve and keep warm.

2 Peel the carrots and parsnips, then continue peeling using a vegetable peeler so that the vegetables form thin slivers.

3 Dice the onion and celery and slice the courgette (zucchini).

4 Sweat the vegetables in the olive oil, starting with the onion and celery, then add the carrot, parsnip and courgette (zucchini).

5 Add the beansprouts and sweetcorn, then the almonds, rice, parsley, pepper and water. Mix well, heat through and serve.

STIR-FRIED VEGETABLES WITH TOASTED CASHEWS (SERVES 4)

Serve with plain boiled rice, millet or quinoa and a side salad.

For a variation, if allowed, dissolve 10 ml (1 dsp) light miso, 10 ml (1 dsp) tomato purée and 20 ml (2 dsp) shoyu/tamari sauce in 285 ml (½ pt/1⅓ cups) of boiling water. Use this instead of the stock. You will not need to add the cornflour (cornstarch) as this produces a delicious thickened sauce.

Choose 6 vegetables from the following:
- 1 onion
- 1 carrot
- 2 sticks (stalks) celery
- ½ pepper
- 2 courgettes (zucchini)
- 12 baby sweetcorn
- 16 sugar snap peas or mangetout
- 115 g (4 oz/1 cup) green beans
- 55 g (2 oz/½ cup) water chestnuts
- 115 g (4oz/1½ cups) red or white cabbage
- 115 g (4oz/2 cups) spinach
- 170 g (6 oz/1½ cups) broccoli or cauliflower florets
- 115 g (4 oz/1 cup) mushrooms

15 ml (1 tbsp) olive oil
15 ml (1 level tbsp) cornflour (cornstarch)
285 ml (½ pint/1 ⅓ cups) good stock
115 g (4 oz/1 cup) toasted cashews

1 Cut the vegetables into shapes that will cook in equal times.
2 Sweat the vegetables in the oil until they begin to soften and brown.
3 Add the stock, cover and cook for a few more minutes.
4 Mix the cornflour (cornstarch) to a smooth paste with a little water and add to the vegetables, stirring all the time. Bring to the boil and simmer until the mixture thickens.
5 Add the cashews and serve.

BRAZILIAN STIR-FRY (SERVES 4)

The almonds need to be very finely ground to thicken the sauce, so shop-bought ones are best. To vary, add 140 g (5 oz/³⁄₄ cup) smoked tofu or cooked chicken instead of one of the vegetables.

55 g (2 oz/¹⁄₃ cup) creamed coconut

Select 6 of the following vegetables:
- 2 onions
- 8 cauliflower florets
- 12 baby sweetcorn
- 2 courgettes (zucchini)
- 55 g (2 oz/¹⁄₂ cup) mangetout
- ¹⁄₂ pepper
- 2 carrots
- 2 sticks (stalks) celery
- 8 broccoli florets

- 55 g (2 oz/¹⁄₂ cup) green beans
- 115 g (4 oz/1 cup) mushrooms
- 115 g (4 oz/1¹⁄₂ cups) white cabbage

15 ml (1 tbsp) olive oil
55 g (2 oz/²⁄₃ cup) ground almonds
3 ml (¹⁄₂ tsp) grated fresh ginger
black pepper
285 ml (¹⁄₂ pint/1¹⁄₃ cups) boiling water
3 ml (¹⁄₂ tsp) dried thyme

1 Dissolve the creamed coconut in the boiling water.
2 Cut the vegetables into pieces that will cook in equal times.
3 Sweat the vegetables in the oil until all are just cooked.
4 Add the coconut water, the ground almonds, the ginger, the thyme and some black pepper. Heat through and serve with rice, millet or another starchy side dish.

BROCCOLI AND SWEETCORN QUICHE (SERVES 4)

Cabbage leaves are used instead of pastry in this quiche. Other ingredients could be used to make quiches, such as tuna fish, prawns, cubed smoked tofu, spinach, mushrooms, courgettes (zucchini) and peppers.

If you cannot eat eggs, try using 425 g (15 oz/1¹⁄₂ cups) of silken tofu and 260 ml (9 fl oz/1¹⁄₄ cups) of soya milk instead of the eggs and milk. The flan will set but will not rise as it would when using eggs.

6–8 large cabbage leaves	455 g (1 lb/8 cups) broccoli florets
2 large onions	10 ml (1 dsp) olive oil
15 ml (1 tbsp) fresh parsley	3 eggs
425 ml (¾ pint/2 cups) soya, rice or almond milk	black pepper
55 g (2 oz/²⁄₃ cup) ground nuts	225 g (8 oz/1 cup) sweetcorn kernels

1 Cook the cabbage and the broccoli in boiling water for approximately 5 minutes until the cabbage leaves are soft enough to line the dish and the broccoli is still crunchy.
2 Cool the broccoli quickly by dipping in cold water to prevent overcooking.
3 Chop the onions and sweat in the oil until they begin to brown and soften. Mix in the parsley.
4 Beat the eggs and milk and season with black pepper.
5 Use the cabbage leaves to double-line a deep 25-cm (10-in) quiche dish.
6 Scatter half the onions over the base, then arrange the broccoli florets around the dish, making sure that they do not come above the top of the dish or they will burn.
7 Fill the gaps between the broccoli with sweetcorn, then scatter the remaining onions over the top. The dish should be well packed with vegetables.
8 Pour over the egg and milk mixture and scatter the ground nuts over the surface.
9 Bake at 400°F/200°C/gas mark 6 for approximately 40–50 minutes or until the centre of the quiche is just setting. Do not overcook or the eggs will start to curdle and spoil the quiche.

CARROT AND LEEK QUICHE (SERVES 4)

If you do not want to use tuna fish or tofu, substitute another vegetable such as green beans, red kidney beans or courgettes (zucchini). If you cannot eat eggs, try using 425 g (15 oz/1½ cups) of silken tofu and 260 ml (9 fl oz/1¼ cups) of soya milk instead of the eggs and milk. The quiche will set but will not rise as it would when using eggs.

For the base:
1 quantity Rice Pancake Mixture (see page 94)

565 g (1¼ lb/5 cups) leeks, sliced	15 ml (1 tbsp) fresh parsley
3 eggs	425 ml (¾ pint/2 cups) soya milk
black pepper	2 medium carrots, grated
200 g (7 oz/1⅓ cups) smoked tofu or tuna fish	55 g (2 oz/⅔ cup) ground nuts

1 Make 4 pancakes using the rice pancake mixture and use to line a greased, deep, 25-cm (10-in) flan dish.
2 Cook the leeks in a little water until they are almost tender. Drain well and mix in the parsley.
3 Beat the eggs with the milk and season with black pepper.
4 Layer half the carrots and leeks in the flan dish and cover with the cubed tofu or drained tuna fish. Repeat with a second layer of carrots and leeks.
5 Pour over the eggs and milk, then sprinkle with the ground nuts.
6 Bake for 40–50 minutes at 400°F/200°C/gas mark 6 until the centre of the flan is just setting. Do not overcook or the eggs will start to curdle.

POTATO, COURGETTE (ZUCCHINI) AND AUBERGINE (EGGPLANT) BAKE (SERVES 4)

If possible, use a food processor to slice the potatoes as this means they will be finely sliced and will cook easily. Tuna fish makes a good substitute for the olives, and sun-dried tomatoes and mushrooms could be used instead of the spinach. Note that the only acceptable sun-dried tomatoes I have found are dried and need soaking to reconstitute. Use carrot juice if you cannot tolerate tomatoes. Serve with salads.

1¼ kg (2½ lb/8 cups) potatoes	2 onions
4 courgettes (zucchini)	1 aubergine (eggplant)
455 g (1 lb/8 cups) spinach	black pepper
1 tin (400 g/15 oz/2 cups) chopped	5 ml (1 tsp) dried oregano
tomatoes in tomato juice	6 sun-dried tomatoes
10 olives, halved	olive oil

1 Finely slice the potatoes and the onion, then cut the courgettes (zucchini) and the aubergine (eggplant) into 2-cm (½-in) slices. Lightly cook the spinach in the water which remains on the leaves after washing.
2 Layer half the potatoes in a large, greased gratin dish or roasting tin. Season with black pepper.
3 Place half the sliced onions on top, then all the aubergine (eggplant) and courgette (zucchini) slices. Season with black pepper.
4 Mix the tinned tomatoes with the oregano and spread on top of the vegetables.
5 Sprinkle the chopped sun-dried tomatoes and the olives over the surface.
6 Cover with a layer of spinach, then the remaining onions and the potatoes.
7 Brush the surface with olive oil and bake in the centre of the oven at 400°F/200°C/gas mark 6 for 1¼ hours. Cover with foil if the potatoes start to brown too much.

POLENTA PIZZA (SERVES 4)

The base will remain soft and will need careful handling when serving. Serve along with a selection of salads. Add a few slivers of goat's cheese to the topping, if allowed.

115 g (4 oz/²⁄₃ cup) polenta	570 ml (l pint/2½ cups) water
or maize meal	15 ml (1 tbsp) olive oil
3 ml (½ tsp) dried oregano	40 ml (2 rounded tbsp) tomato
olive oil for dribbling on the surface	purée

Toppings to choose from:
- sliced peppers
- sliced spring onions (scallions)
- sweetcorn kernels
- sliced mushrooms
- black or green olives
- pine nuts
- tuna fish
- sardines
- finely sliced onion
- sliced tomatoes
- artichoke hearts
- sliced courgettes (zucchini)
- sun-dried tomatoes
- pineapple
- prawns
- garlic

1 Mix the polenta or maize meal with 140 ml (¼ pt/²/₃ cup) cold water in a pan (preferably non-stick). Add 425 ml (¾ pint/2 cups) of boiling water, mixing as you add.
2 Bring to the boil and simmer over a low heat, stirring constantly for 5 minutes. The mixture should be thick and smooth. Beat in the olive oil.
3 Grease a 30-cm (10–12-in) pizza pan or similar sized baking tray, and spread the hot mixture over the surface to form a pizza base.
4 Spread the tomato purée on top and sprinkle with oregano.
5 Add the toppings of your choice, making sure you build up a substantial layer.
6 Drizzle the surface with olive oil and bake in a preheated oven at 400°F/200°C/gas mark 6 for 30–35 minutes.

ONION AND HERB BREAD PIZZA

Use the ingredients for Onion and Herb Loaf *(see Chapter 9, page 158)* to make a pizza base. The flavourings can be omitted if you prefer a plain base. Bake for 10 minutes, then remove the base from the oven. Spread tomato purée and oregano over the surface, then add your chosen topping (see previous recipe). Return to the oven and bake for a further 10–15 minutes or until the base is brown around the edges and the topping is cooked.

VEGETABLE LASAGNE (SERVES 4)

If you cannot tolerate corn, try using cooked rice pancakes instead of the Polenta Lasagne. Those who can eat cheese could sprinkle a little on the surface before cooking.

Lasagne

115 g (4 oz/⅔ cup) polenta   570 ml water (1 pint/2½ cups)
15 ml (1 tbsp) olive oil

Filling

3 onions   2 courgettes (zucchini)
2 sticks (stalks) celery   1 carrot
10 ml (1 dsp) olive oil   3 ml (½ tsp) dried basil
3 ml (½ tsp) dried oregano   30 ml (2 tbsp) tomato purée
60 ml (2 fl oz/¼ cup) water   10 black olives
6 sun-dried tomatoes

White sauce

30 ml (2 level tbsp) cornflour (cornstarch)   425 ml (¾ pint/2 cups) soya, rice
5 ml (1 tsp) mustard   or almond milk
black pepper   2 ml (¼ tsp) nutmeg

1 Mix the polenta with 140 ml (¼ pint/½ cup) of cold water in a pan. Add 425 ml (¾ pint/2 cups) of boiling water, mixing as you add. Bring to the boil and cook for 5 minutes, stirring constantly. Add the olive oil and mix well.
2 Grease a baking tray twice the size of the dish you intend to use for the lasagne. Spread the polenta onto the baking tray making a thin sheet. Allow to cool and cut in half, then use the sheets of polenta instead of lasagne.
3 To make the filling, dice the onions, courgettes (zucchini), celery and carrot and chop the sun-dried tomatoes. Sweat the vegetables in the olive oil until they begin to soften. Add the remaining filling ingredients and mix well.
4 To make the white sauce, mix the cornflour (cornstarch) with the mustard and a little milk in a saucepan until smooth. Add

the remaining sauce ingredients and bring to the boil, stirring constantly.

5 To assemble the lasagne, place half the vegetable mixture into a gratin or lasagne dish and cover with a sheet of polenta. Repeat with the remaining vegetables and polenta. Pour the white sauce over the surface.

6 Bake for approximately 40 minutes at 400°F/200°C/gas mark 6.

Seafood Lasagne

Use tuna fish and prawns instead of the olives and sun-dried tomatoes in the above recipe.

Lentil Lasagne

Use the Lentil Bolognese recipe *(see page 90)* instead of the vegetable mixture in the above recipe.

STUFFED BAKED POTATOES (SERVES 4)

4 large baking potatoes   filling (see below)

1 Wash the potatoes and prick the skins to prevent bursting.
2 Bake for 1¼ hours in the centre of the oven at 400°F/200°C/gas mark 6.
3 When cooked, split the potatoes in half and roughly mash by pressing a fork into the flesh. Pile one of the following fillings into the centre.

Mushroom and Tomato Filling

Sauté 170 g (6 oz/1½ cups) of sliced mushrooms in a little oil, add the diced flesh of 4 skinned tomatoes and 12 quartered olives. Heat through but do not cook or the tomatoes will become too soft.

Tuna, Celery and Egg or Avocado Filling

Mix a tin of drained tuna fish (200 g/7 oz/1⅓ cups) with 2 diced hardboiled eggs (or 1 avocado), 2 large sticks (stalks) celery diced and 80 ml (4 tbsp) mayonnaise.

Tahini and Tomato Filling

Scoop the flesh out of the potatoes and mash in a bowl with 60 ml (4 tbsp) of tahini, the flesh of 4 tomatoes skinned and diced and 10 ml (1 dsp) of tomato purée. Pile back into the potato shells and sprinkle the surface with sunflower seeds.

Chicken or Butterbean in White Sauce Filling

Make a White Sauce *(see Chapter 8, page 145)* and add 170 g (6 oz/1¼ cups) of cooked chicken (or cooked butter beans), 55 g (2 oz/¼ cup) of frozen peas and 15 ml (1 tbsp) of fresh chopped herbs, such as parsley, tarragon or coriander.

Prawns with Sweetcorn and Celery Filling

Mix 115 g (4 oz/1 cup) of prawns with 55 g (2 oz/¼ cup) of sweetcorn kernels or peas, 2 large sticks (stalks) of celery diced and 80 ml (4 rounded tbsp) of mayonnaise.

Other fillings which could be used include houmous, ratatouille, Lentil Bolognese *(see page 90)*, Avocado and Cashew Nut Pâté *(see Chapter 2, page 61)*, coleslaw, Tropical Curried Chicken Salad *(see Chapter 4, page 88)* or Minted Avocado and Chickpea Salad *(see Chapter 4, page 83)*.

WINTER BEAN AND TOFU CASSEROLE
(SERVES 4)

This is a delicious casserole for a cold winter's day. Serve it along with rice, millet, quinoa or baked potatoes and a salad, or crusty garlic bread, if allowed. Omit the tofu if not tolerated and substitute another vegetable or different beans. For extra flavour, 15 ml (1 tbsp) of shoyu/tamari sauce can be added.

1 whole corn on the cob	½ small swede
1 large parsnip	2 medium onions
2 carrots	2 courgettes (zucchini)
170 g (6 oz/1 cup) plain tofu	225 g (8 oz/1 ⅓ cups) cooked red
3 ml (½ tsp) dried thyme	kidney beans
3 ml (½ tsp) dried rosemary	1 bay leaf
black pepper	425 ml (15 fl oz/2 cups) water
285 ml (10 fl oz/1 ⅓ cups) soya	30 ml (2 level tbsp) cornflour
or almond milk	(cornstarch)

1 Cut the corn on the cob into 2-cm (½-in) sections.
2 Cut the vegetables into chunks, adjusting the size according to how quickly they will cook. Place all the vegetables into a casserole dish.
3 Cube the tofu and add to the casserole along with the kidney beans, herbs, pepper and water. Mix gently.
4 Cover the casserole and cook for 1 hour at 400°F/200°C/gas mark 6. There should be only a small amount of liquid left in the casserole but watch to make sure it does not dry up altogether.
5 When cooked, lift out the vegetables and tofu using a slotted spoon, and remove the bay leaf.
6 Mix the soya or almond milk to a smooth paste with the cornflour (cornstarch) and add to the juices in the casserole dish. Bring to the boil on top of the cooker, stirring constantly, and simmer for 2 minutes. Return the vegetables to the pan and gently mix.

BEAN AND VEGETABLE CASSEROLE
(SERVES 4)

Serve with rice, millet, quinoa or baked potatoes and a salad. Those allowed could use crusty bread to mop up the juices.

A variety of casseroles can be made by substituting other ingredients. Use carrot juice or other vegetable juice instead of the tomatoes. Use other herbs instead of the cumin and coriander, such as 5 ml (1 tsp) of dill seeds, 5 ml (1 tsp) of fennel and 3 ml (½ tsp) of marjoram. Substitute other vegetables, such as peppers, leeks, fennel, cauliflower, kohlrabi, turnip and celeriac. Buckwheat could be used instead of the beans to produce a buckwheat and vegetable casserole. Cook the buckwheat first for 12 minutes in lots of water, then drain and add to the casserole.

Extra flavour can be added for those allowed by including 5 ml (1 tsp) of miso dissolved in a little boiling water or 15 ml (1 tbsp) of shoyu/tamari sauce.

55 g (2 oz/⅓ cup) red split lentils	1 tin (400 g/15 oz/2 cups)
1 clove garlic	chopped tomatoes in juice
5 ml (1 tsp) grated ginger	5 ml (1 tsp) paprika
5 ml (1 tsp) ground cumin	5 ml (1 tsp) ground coriander
black pepper	1 bay leaf
1 onion	1 large carrot
1 parsnip	2 sticks (stalks) celery
2 courgettes (zucchini)	115 g (4 oz/1 cup) green beans
8 broccoli florets	170 g (6 oz/1 cup) cooked beans
285 ml (½ pt/1⅓ cups) water	(chickpeas, black eye, kidney, etc

1 Place the lentils, the tomatoes, the pressed garlic clove, the ginger, the herbs and the spices in a casserole dish and mix.
2 Chop the vegetables into chunks, varying the size according to how quickly they will cook. Place on top of the lentil mix along with the cooked beans.
3 Pour the water over the ingredients but do not mix at this stage. The lentils need to stay at the bottom of the casserole in the liquid in order to cook.

4 Cover the casserole and bake in the centre of the oven at 400°F/200°C/gas mark 6 for 1 hour, mixing gently half-way through. Remove the bay leaf before serving.

BROCCOLI AND SMOKED TOFU BAKE (SERVES 4)

If tofu is not tolerated, try substituting tuna fish, cooked chicken, chopped hardboiled eggs or another vegetable.

1 medium onion	225 g (8 oz/4 cups) broccoli florets
30 ml (2 level tbsp) rice flour	285 ml (½ pt/1 ⅓ cups) soya milk
2 ml (¼ tsp) nutmeg	3 ml (½ tsp) lemon rind
black pepper	225 g (8 oz/1½ cups) cooked
225 g (8 oz/1¼ cups) smoked tofu	red kidney beans

Topping:

85 g (3 oz/1 cup) millet flakes	30 g (1 oz/¹⁄₆ cup) brown rice flour
55 g (2 oz/²⁄₃ cup) ground nuts e.g. almonds, hazelnuts	20 ml (2 dsp) sunflower oil
	30 ml (2 tbsp) sunflower seeds

1 Chop the onion and cook with the broccoli in 140 ml (¼ pt/²⁄₃ cup) of boiling water until just tender. Drain and keep the cooking liquid.
2 Put the rice flour in a pan and mix to a smooth paste using a little soya milk. Add the remaining soya milk and the stock from the vegetables made up to 140 ml (¼ pt/²⁄₃ cup) with water.
3 Bring to the boil, stirring constantly, then lower the heat and simmer for 2 minutes.
4 Add the nutmeg, lemon rind and pepper, then the vegetables, beans and the tofu which should be cubed.
5 Spoon the mixture into a large gratin dish (or 4 small dishes).
6 To make the topping, place the millet flakes, rice flour and ground nuts in a bowl and rub in the oil by hand.
7 Spread the topping over the vegetable and tofu mixture and scatter the sunflower seeds over the surface.

8 Bake for 15 minutes or until the topping is brown at 400°F/ 200°C/gas mark 6 on the top shelf of the oven.

VEGETABLE CRUMBLE (SERVES 4)

Follow the previous recipe but substitute a 680-g (1½-lb/6–8-cup) selection of vegetables instead of the tofu and kidney beans – try leeks, parsnips, carrots, celery, courgettes (zucchini), etc. Cook all the vegetables together in just over 140 ml (¼ pint/⅔ cup) of water and add 3 ml (½ tsp) of dried rosemary and 3 ml (½ tsp) of dried thyme to the sauce. Keep the remaining ingredients the same and cook for 15 minutes, as above.

VEGETABLE AND CASHEW NUT MEDLEY (SERVES 4)

Serve in individual gratin dishes or as a sauce to go with rice or pasta. Accompany with salads.

Other vegetables which substitute well in this dish include onions, baby sweetcorn, water chestnuts, mangetout or sugar snap peas. Try walnuts or toasted slivered almonds instead of the cashews. If it is tolerated, add 15 ml (1 tbsp) of shoyu/tamari sauce to the sauce ingredients.

170 g (6 oz/3 cups) broccoli florets	85 g (3 oz/¾ cup) green beans
1 courgette (zucchini)	1–2 sticks (stalks) celery
½ red pepper	1 leek
1 medium carrot	115 g (4 oz/1 cup) whole cashews

Sauce

5 ml (1 tsp) tomato purée	5 ml (1 tsp) grated ginger
10 ml (1 dsp) lemon juice	3 ml (½ tsp) grated lemon rind
30 ml (2 tbsp) orange juice	2 ml (¼ tsp) nutmeg
5 ml (1 tsp) paprika	15 ml (1 tbsp) fresh coriander
15 ml (1 tbsp) cornflour (cornstarch)	340 ml (12 fl oz/1½ cups) stock (use vegetable cooking liquid and water)

1 Cut the beans in half and slice the courgette (zucchini), celery, red pepper and leek. Cut the carrot into matchstick pieces. Toast the cashews.
2 Place the vegetables in a pan with 285 ml (10 fl oz/1^1/$_3$ cups) boiling water. Bring to the boil and simmer for 5 minutes or until the vegetables are just cooked but slightly crisp. Drain, keeping the liquid for stock.
3 To make the sauce, place all the sauce ingredients except the stock in a pan and mix to a smooth paste. Add the stock gradually.
4 Bring to the boil, stirring constantly, and simmer for 2 minutes. Add the vegetables and cashew nuts to the sauce and allow to heat through.

POTATO AND PARSNIP PIE CRUST

Potatoes and parsnips are used to make a pie crust which can then be filled with one of the following fillings or one of your choice.

455 g (1 lb/3 ^{1}/$_4$ cups) potatoes	340 g (^{3}/$_4$ lb/2 ^{1}/$_3$ cups) parsnips
black pepper	olive oil for brushing

1 Cut the potatoes and parsnips into equal sized chunks and cook together in boiling water until tender.
2 Sieve, and save the cooking liquid.
3 Mash the potatoes and the parsnips with some black pepper and sufficient cooking liquid to make them soft and smooth.
4 Press into a greased 23-cm (9-in) pie dish, moulding with the fingers to form a pie shape. Brush the surface with olive oil and bake in the oven for 45 minutes at 400°F/200°C/gas mark 6.

Spinach and Egg Filling (serves 4)

4 hardboiled eggs	455 g (1 lb/8 cups) spinach
425 ml (^{3}/$_4$ pint/2 cups) White Sauce	paprika
(see Chapter 8, page 145)	

1 Halve the hardboiled eggs and lay cut side down into the pie.
2 Shred the spinach and then cook in the water in which it has

been washed for no more than 5 minutes or until it is soft and wilted. Drain and spread over the eggs.

3 Make the White Sauce as directed and pour over the eggs and spinach. Sprinkle with paprika and serve.

Ratatouille Filling (serves 4)

Add 55 g (2 oz/½ cup) of toasted pine nuts and a few chopped olives and sun-dried tomatoes to the basic Ratatouille recipe *(see Chapter 8, page 147)*. Fill the pie and serve.

Stir-fried Vegetable Filling (serves 4)

Stir-fry a 680-g (1½-lb/6–8-cup) selection of vegetables, pile into the pie and serve. Sprinkle with toasted sunflower seeds or a little grated cheese, if allowed.

STUFFED PEPPERS (SERVES 4)

Serve as a vegetarian main course with potatoes and salad or as a vegetable accompaniment. Peppers could also be stuffed with Nut Roast *(see page 97)* or Millet and Walnut Bake *(see page 92)* ingredients.

1 onion	1 clove garlic
10 ml (1 dsp) olive oil	225 g (8 oz/1 ⅓ cups) cooked rice
20 ml (2 dsp) raisins (optional)	30 ml (2 tbsp) pine nuts or
55 g (2 oz/¼ cup) sweetcorn kernels	cashew nuts
or frozen peas	10 ml (1 dsp) fresh chopped mint
10 ml (1 dsp) fresh chopped parsley	3 ml (½ tsp) ground cinnamon
black pepper	4 medium green peppers

1 Chop the onion and sweat along with the pressed clove of garlic until they begin to soften and brown.
2 Add all the remaining ingredients except the peppers and mix well.
3 Cut a circular hole in the top of each pepper, removing the stalk. Use a spoon to scoop out internal fibres and seeds.

4 Hold each of the peppers in turn over the pan containing the stuffing mixture. Using a spoon, fill each pepper with the mixture and press it down well.

5 Place the peppers in a deep-sided ovenproof dish. Cut a little off the base of the peppers, if necessary, to enable them to stand easily.

6 Pour 140 ml (¼ pint/²⁄₃ cup) of water around the peppers and cover with foil. Bake in the centre of the oven at 400°F/200°C/gas mark 6 for 50–60 minutes or until the peppers are soft but not mushy.

STUFFED AUBERGINES (EGGPLANTS) (SERVES 4)

Serve with salad and vegetables as a main course or individually as starters.

Millet or quinoa could be used instead of the rice. The original recipe used 115 g (4 oz/2 cups) breadcrumbs instead of the rice and ground almonds. If permitted, try this for a variation. Half a tin of flaked tuna fish (100 g/3½ oz/½ cup) or 30 ml (2 tbsp) grated cheese can be added for extra flavour, if allowed, and the olives could be omitted. Meat-eaters will begin to think vegetarian after eating this.

2 large aubergines (eggplants)	1 onion
1 clove garlic	5 ml (1 tsp) olive oil
4 medium tomatoes	12 black olives
5 ml (1 tsp) tomato purée	3 ml (½ tsp) dried marjoram
3 ml (½ tsp) dried oregano	10 ml (1 dsp) fresh chopped parsley
10 ml (1 dsp) fresh chopped coriander	black pepper
55 g (2 oz/¹⁄₃ cup) cooked rice	55 g (2 oz/²⁄₃ cup) ground
olive oil for drizzling on the surface	almonds

1 Cut the aubergines (eggplants) in half and scoop out the flesh leaving 2 cm (½ in) around the edge next to the skin. Dice the flesh finely and place in a large bowl.

2 Finely dice the onion and press the garlic clove. Sweat the onion and garlic in 5 ml (1 tsp) of olive oil until they begin to soften and brown. Add these to the diced aubergine (eggplant) flesh in the bowl.

3 Skin the tomatoes and dice the flesh. Quarter the black olives. Add to the bowl along with the remaining ingredients and mix.

4 Place the aubergine (eggplant) shells on a baking tray, in a gratin dish or in individual dishes.

5 Pile the stuffing into the shells, pressing down firmly.

6 Drizzle the surface with olive oil, cover with foil and bake at 400°F/200°C/gas mark 6 for 1 hour until the aubergines (eggplants) are quite soft.

STUFFED MARROW

Use the recipe for Stuffed Aubergines to make stuffed marrow. Peel the marrow, cut into 4-cm (1½-in) slices and remove the centres. The centres can be finely diced and added to the filling ingredients unless the marrows are old and full of seeds. If this is the case, use another length of marrow to chop up for the filling. Bake for approximately ½ hour.

RICE WITH SWEETCORN AND COCONUT
(SERVES 4)

Serve as a side dish.

225 g (4 oz/½ cup) sweetcorn kernels or frozen peas
90 ml (3 fl oz/⅓ cup) water
225 g (8 oz/1½ cups) cooked rice

30 g (1 oz/⅙ cup) creamed coconut
30 ml (3 dsp) desiccated coconut

1 Break the sweetcorn kernels (or peas) in a bowl with a fork.

2 Dissolve the creamed coconut in the boiling water.

3 Add all the ingredients to the pan and bring slowly to the boil, stirring frequently.

4 Turn off the heat and leave to stand, covered, for 5 minutes.

CARROT AND COCONUT RICE (SERVES 4)

Serve as a side dish.

30 g (1 oz/¹/₆ cup) creamed coconut
5 cardamom pods or 3 ml (½ tsp)
   ground cardamom
225 g (8 oz/1¹/₃ cups) carrots, grated

90 ml (3 fl oz/¹/₃ cup) boiling water
3 ml (½ tsp) ground nutmeg
225 g (8 oz/1½ cups) cooked rice

1 Dissolve the creamed coconut in the boiling water. If using cardamom pods, split the pods and remove the seeds, throwing away the empty shells.
2 Place all the ingredients into a pan and bring slowly to the boil, stirring frequently.
3 Cover and simmer for 4–5 minutes, or until the carrots are cooked.

SUSHI

2 sheets sushi nori
   (toasted dried seaweed)

1 portion rice with sweetcorn or
   carrot and coconut rice

1 Lay the sheets of nori on a flat surface and divide the rice between them. Spread the rice out, pressing it down and keeping it 3 cm (1 in) away from the farthest and nearest edges.
2 Roll up the nori sheets like a Swiss roll, dampening the farthest edge so that it sticks to itself and seals the roll.
3 Allow to cool. Cut the sushi roll into 3-cm (1-in) slices to serve as snacks or cut into 8-cm (3-in) lengths to serve with vegetables or salads.

Indian Food

Indian food fits very well into this eating regime. It is an ideal way to entertain as a wide selection of dishes can be offered, most of which are allowed. Try the following four dishes but also include the Chicken Curry (see page 123), the Spicy Baked Chicken (see page 126) or the Lamb Korma (see page 130) from Chapter 6. Add a few salads from Chapter 4 as curry accompaniments, such as Apple, Carrot and Ginger (see page 81); Cucumber, Mint and Yogurt (see page 81 or Tomato and Coriander (see page 81) and some naan bread or poppadoms for those allowed wheat. With food like this, who would mind being on a special diet?

VEGETABLE MASALA (SERVES 4)

680-g (1½-lb/6–8-cup) selection of vegetables, such as:

- cauliflower florets
- leeks
- carrots
- broccoli
- celery
- onions
- courgettes (zucchini)
- parsnips
- green beans
- sweetcorn

15 ml (1 tbsp) olive oil
3 ml (½ tsp) ground cumin
2 ml (¼ tsp) ground cardamom
3 ml (½ tsp) tumeric
285 ml (½ pt/1 ⅓ cups) water
15 ml (1 tbsp) lemon juice
55 g (2 oz/⅔ cup) ground almonds

5 ml (1 tsp) garam masala
3 ml (½ tsp) ground coriander
3 ml (½ tsp) fennel seeds
55 g (2 oz/⅓ cup) creamed coconut
5 ml (1 tsp) grated ginger

1 Cut the vegetables into shapes which will cook in roughly equal times. Sweat the vegetables in the olive oil until they begin to soften and brown.
2 Add the spices to the pan and sweat for another 2 minutes.
3 Dissolve the coconut in the boiling water and add to the vegetables along with the lemon juice, ginger and ground almonds. Stir to mix.

4 Simmer for another few minutes until all the vegetables are just cooked. Add a little more water if the mixture starts to become too dry. Serve with rice, millet or quinoa.

BIRIANI WITH RICE (SERVES 4)

Serve with plain boiled rice.

2 onions	2 medium baking apples
1 clove garlic	55 g (2 oz/^{1}/$_3$ cup) split red lentils
55 g (2 oz/^{1}/$_3$ cup) creamed coconut	850 ml (1^1/$_2$ pints/3^3/$_4$ cups) water
10 ml (1 dsp) tomato purée (optional)	5 ml (1 tsp) ground fennel
3 ml (^{1}/$_2$ tsp) ground cardamom	5 ml (1 tsp) ground cumin
5 ml (1 tsp) ground coriander	5 ml (1 tsp) tumeric
5 ml (1 tsp) garam masala	5 ml (1 tsp) grated ginger
55 g (2 oz/^{2}/$_3$ cup) ground almonds	

1 Finely dice the onions, grate the baking apples and press the garlic clove. Wash the red lentils.
2 Place all the ingredients in a saucepan, bring to the boil and simmer gently for 30–40 minutes until the lentils disintegrate to form part of the sauce. Stir occasionally while cooking.

QUICK BEAN CURRY (SERVES 4)

Use tinned beans for quickness, washing the beans well to remove the salt.

55 g (2 oz/^{1}/$_3$ cup) creamed coconut	285 ml (^{1}/$_2$ pt/1 ^{1}/$_3$ cups) boiling water
^{1}/$_2$ pepper, diced	
85 g (3 oz/^{1}/$_3$ cup) sweetcorn or peas	1 onion, diced
225 g (8 oz/1 ^{1}/$_3$ cups) cooked beans (e.g. chickpeas, butterbeans)	1 tin (400 g/15 oz/2 cups) chopped tomatoes in tomato juice
1 clove garlic, pressed	5 ml (1 tsp) grated ginger
5 ml (1 tsp) ground coriander	5 ml (1 tsp) ground cumin
15 ml (1 tbsp) fresh chopped coriander	

1   Dissolve the coconut in the boiling water in a saucepan.
2   Add the remaining ingredients, bring to the boil and simmer for 15 minutes. Serve with rice, millet or quinoa.

MUSHROOM CURRY

Add 340 g (12 oz/3 cups) of small button mushrooms instead of the beans to the previous recipe.

VEGETABLE ROGAN JOSH (SERVES 4)

I like to select just two or three vegetables and make, for instance, a cauliflower and courgette rogan josh or an okra, baby sweetcorn and fennel rogan josh. The variations are endless.

6 medium onions
15 ml (1 tbsp) olive oil
5 ml (1 tsp) ground coriander
5 ml (1 tsp) ground cumin
5 ml (1 tsp) garam masala
3 ml (½ tsp) tumeric
5 ml (1 tsp) grated ginger

2 cloves garlic
570 ml (1 pint/2½ cups) creamed tomatoes or tomato juice
5 ml (1 tsp) fennel seeds
5 ml (1 tsp) paprika
2 ml (¼ tsp) cardamom, ground or seeds

680 g (1½ lb/6–8 cups) vegetables e.g. carrots, celery, peppers, mushrooms, fennel, okra, baby sweetcorn, broccoli, courgettes (zucchini)

1   Dice the onions and press the garlic cloves. Sweat the onions and garlic gently in the olive oil until they are a golden brown colour. This will take at least ½ hour. Do not rush, do not turn the heat up too high and stir frequently.
2   Make the creamed tomato juice up to 850 ml (1½ pints/3¾ cups) with water.
3   Blend half of the onions with half of the tomato juice in a food processor until they are smooth and creamy.
4   Add the spices to the pan with the remaining onions, and continue to sweat for 2–3 minutes, stirring constantly.
5   Add the onion and tomato mixture, the remaining tomato juice, the ginger and the vegetables cut into chunks. Stir to mix.

6 Bring to the boil and simmer for 15–20 minutes or until the vegetables are just cooked. Serve with rice, millet or quinoa.

VEGETABLE AND FRUIT ROGAN JOSH

Try adding ½ diced mango, 1 sliced banana or ½ cup of chopped pineapple just before the vegetables have finished cooking.

Meat Dishes

CHICKEN POLO (SERVES 4)

2 onions
1 large carrot
55 g (2 oz/¼ cup) dried apricots
10 ml (1 dsp) olive oil
1 cinnamon stick or 3 ml (½ tsp)
   ground cinnamon
black pepper
30 ml (1 heaped tbsp) raisins (optional)
55 g (2 oz/½ cup) split almonds

1 clove garlic
225 g (8 oz/1 cup) chicken
   breasts, diced
285 g (10 oz/1¼ cups) short-grain
   rice
1 bay leaf
710 ml (1¼ pints/3¼ cups) stock
   or water

1 Chop the onion, press the garlic and cut the carrot into match-stick pieces. Cut the apricots into small dice.
2 Sweat the onion and the garlic in the oil until they begin to brown. Use a heavy-bottomed pan with a good-fitting lid.
3 Add the chicken and sauté for a few minutes until it starts to brown. Wash the rice well and add, along with the remaining ingredients (except the almonds).
4 Bring to the boil and simmer gently for 40–50 minutes until the rice is cooked. A little more water or stock may be needed near to the end of the cooking time to prevent the mixture sticking to the pan. The rice should be creamy and sticky when cooked.
5 Toast the almonds and stir in just before serving.

CHICKEN CURRY (SERVES 4)

1 large onion
¼ green pepper
225 g (8 oz/1 cup) cooked chicken
5 ml (1 tsp) hot madras curry powder
570 ml (1 pint/2½ cups) water or stock
15 ml (1 tbsp) tomato purée, optional
10 ml (1 level dsp) cornflour (cornstarch)

1 stick (stalk) celery
¼ red pepper
1 large baking apple
1 clove garlic
15 ml (1 tbsp) desiccated coconut
black pepper

1 Dice the onion, celery, peppers and the chicken and grate the baking apple. Press the garlic clove.
2 Place all the ingredients except the cornflour (cornstarch) into a saucepan, bring to the boil and simmer for 50 minutes, stirring occasionally.
3 Mix the cornflour (cornstarch) in a little water and stir into the curry to thicken. Reheat and cook for 2 minutes before serving.

CHICKEN BRAZILIAN (SERVES 4)

3–4 chicken breasts
15 ml (1 tbsp) olive oil
2 cloves garlic
55 g (2 oz/⅓ cup) creamed coconut
55 g (2 oz/⅔ cup) ground almonds
black pepper

15 ml (1 tbsp) lemon juice
2 onions
1 green pepper
140 ml (¼ pt/⅔ cup) boiling water
2 large tomatoes
15 ml (1 tbsp) parsley

1 Cube the chicken, toss in the lemon juice and sweat in the olive oil until beginning to brown.
2 Chop the onions, press the garlic cloves and add to the chicken. Sweat for a further 5 minutes.
3 Slice the green pepper, dissolve the creamed coconut in the boiling water and skin and chop the tomatoes. Add to the pan along with the ground almonds and black pepper.
4 Stir, bring to the boil and simmer for 15 minutes, adding a little more liquid if the mixture starts to become too dry.
5 Add the parsley and serve with plain boiled rice, millet or quinoa.

CHICKEN CASSEROLE (SERVES 4)

1 onion	55 g (2 oz/½ cup) mushrooms
1 stick (stalk) celery	(optional)
¼ green pepper	2 carrots
1 clove garlic	285 ml (½ pint/1 ⅓ cups) water
10 ml (1 dsp) tomato purée	3 ml (½ tsp) dried marjoram
(optional)	3 ml (½ tsp) dried rosemary
3 ml (½ tsp) paprika	2 ml (¼ tsp) dried sage
1 bay leaf	black pepper
5 ml (1 tsp) cornflour (cornstarch)	4 chicken joints (skinned)

1 Cut the vegetables into bite-sized pieces and add to the casserole along with the pressed garlic.
2 Mix together the water, tomato purée, herbs and seasoning and pour over the vegetables.
3 Add the chicken pieces, cover the casserole and cook at 400°F/ 200°C/gas mark 6 for approximately 1¼ hours or until the chicken is tender.
4 Stir the cornflour (cornstarch) in a little water and add to the casserole to thicken it. Reheat and remove the bay leaf.
5 Serve with rice and a green salad or fresh vegetables.

STIR-FRIED CHICKEN AND VEGETABLES (SERVES 4)

An alternative sauce can be made, for those allowed the following, by mixing 10 ml (1 dsp) tomato purée, 10 ml (1 dsp) light miso and 20 ml (2 dsp) shoyu sauce/tamari with 285 ml (½ pint/1⅓ cups) of water. Add this instead of the stock and cornflour (cornstarch).

Select 3–4 vegetables from the following:
- 2 courgettes (zucchini)
- 55 g (4 oz/1 cup) mangetout
- 115 g (2 oz/½ cup) water chestnuts
- 115 g (4 oz/2 cups) broccoli florets
- 1 onion, sliced
- ½ red pepper
- 2 carrots
- 8 baby sweetcorn
- 55 g (2 oz/½ cup) mushrooms

1 clove garlic, pressed	15 ml (1 tbsp) olive oil
285 ml (½ pt/1 ⅓ cups) stock or water	2 chicken breasts
10 ml (1 dsp) cornflour (cornstarch)	black pepper

1 Cut the vegetables into pieces that will cook in approximately the same amount of time.
2 Sweat the vegetables and garlic in the olive oil for a few minutes. Add the chicken and sweat for 5 minutes.
3 Mix the stock to a smooth paste with the cornflour (cornstarch), and add to the vegetables and meat.
4 Bring to the boil and simmer for approximately 5 minutes until the vegetables and chicken are cooked.
5 Season with black pepper and serve with boiled rice and salads.

CHICKEN WITH BARBECUE SAUCE
(SERVES 4)

30 ml (2 tbsp) lemon juice	30 ml (2 tbsp) tomato purée
5 ml (1 tsp) Chinese five spice powder	1 clove garlic, pressed
140 ml (¼ pint/⅔ cup) apple juice	140 ml (¼ pint/⅔ cup) stock or
4 chicken breasts	water
10 ml (1 dsp) cornflour (cornstarch)	

1 Mix all the ingredients except the chicken and the cornflour (cornstarch) to form a smooth sauce. Marinade the chicken in the sauce for at least 2 hours.
2 Remove the chicken from the marinade, place on a greased baking tray in the centre of the oven at 400°C/200°C/gas mark 6 for 30 minutes. Baste with the juices from the chicken once during cooking.
3 Mix the cornflour (cornstarch) to a smooth paste in a pan with a little of the marinade. Add the remaining marinade and any juices from the cooked chicken. Bring to the boil, stirring constantly, and allow to simmer for 2 minutes.
4 Serve the chicken on a bed of rice with the sauce poured over.

SPICY BAKED CHICKEN (SERVES 4)

If allowed, a little yogurt could be mixed with any cooking juices from the chicken and served as an accompaniment.

Use foil to cover the baking tray to make washing-up easier.

2 cloves garlic	60 ml (4 tbsp) lemon juice
2 ml (¼ tsp) black pepper	10 ml (1 level dsp) paprika
10 ml (1 level dsp) ground cumin	2 ml (¼ tsp) cayenne pepper
10 ml (1 dsp) tumeric	4 chicken breasts or chicken
parsley to garnish	portions, skinned

1 Combine all the ingredients except the chicken. Rub the spice mixture into the chicken pieces and leave to marinade for at least 3 hours in a covered container.
2 Place the chicken pieces on a baking tray, cover with foil and bake in the centre of the oven at 400°C/200°C/gas mark 6 for 30 minutes if using chicken breasts and 1 hour if using joints.
3 Serve sprinkled with parsley, accompanied by brown rice and dahl *(see Chapter 8, page 148)* and with a salad or fresh vegetables.

SIMA'S CHICKEN (SERVES 4)

Omit the raisins if you cannot tolerate dried fruit.

225 g (8 oz/1⅙ cups) brown rice	340 g (12 oz/2¼ cups) cooked
2 carrots	chicken
rind of ½ orange	juice of 1 orange
60 ml (3 tbsp) raisins (optional)	black pepper
115 g (4 oz/1 cup) toasted flaked almonds	

1 Cook the brown rice and keep warm.
2 Cut the chicken into bite-sized pieces or into small joints.
3 Cut the carrots into matchstick pieces. Thinly pare the orange rind and cut into matchstick strips.

4 Cook the carrots in the orange juice with the orange rind and raisins for approximately 5 minutes until just cooked. Warm the chicken.
5 Mix together the rice, the chicken, the carrot mixture (including any remaining cooking liquid), the black pepper and the nuts, and serve.

CHICKEN LIVER RISOTTO (SERVES 4)

If you cannot use mushrooms, try substituting two finely sliced courgettes (zucchini). Use organic chicken livers, if possible.

225 g (8 oz/1 ¹⁄₆ cups) brown rice
225 g (8 oz/2 cups) mushrooms
15 ml (1 tbsp) olive oil
3 ml (½ tsp) dried basil

3 medium onions
225 g (8 oz/1 cup) chicken livers
black pepper

1 Cook the rice and keep warm.
2 Chop the onions, slice the mushrooms and cut the chicken livers into small pieces.
3 In a large frying pan or wok, sweat the onions in the oil until they begin to soften and brown.
4 Turn the heat full on, add the mushrooms and stir-fry for 2 minutes.
5 Add the chicken livers, black pepper and basil, and stir-fry until the mixture begins to brown and the liver is just cooked. This will only take a few minutes.
6 Add the rice, mix well and serve with salad and vegetables.

RABBIT OR CHICKEN WITH PRUNES
(SERVES 4)

Accompany with brown rice, millet or quinoa and with salads or vegetables.

8 whole prunes
5 ml (1 tsp) dried sage
2 ml (¼ tsp) chilli powder
10 ml (1 dsp) tomato purée
1 carrot cut into matchsticks
2 onions, chopped
2 large sticks (stalks) celery, sliced
10 ml (1 dsp) cornflour (cornstarch)
10 ml (1 dsp) lemon juice

10 ml (1 dsp) paprika
5 ml (1 tsp) dried thyme
4 rabbit or chicken portions
425 ml (¾ pint/2 cups) water or stock (including liquid in which prunes were soaked)
black pepper
1 bay leaf

1 Soak the prunes for 2–3 hrs in water which has been brought to the boil.
2 Mix the paprika, sage, thyme and chilli. Skin the meat and toss in the spices until it is coated all over. Place in a casserole dish.
3 Mix the tomato purée with the stock and the lemon juice and add to the casserole along with the vegetables, prunes, pepper and bay leaf.
4 Cook slowly in the oven at 370°C/185°C/gas mark 4 for approximately 2 hours.
5 Mix the cornflour (cornstarch) with a little water and stir into the casserole. Bring to the boil and cook for 2 minutes before serving.

LAMB WITH ORANGE AND GINGER SAUCE
(SERVES 4)

Serve with brown rice, millet or quinoa and vegetables or salads.

10 ml (1 dsp) tomato purée
3 ml (½ tsp) dried ginger
3 ml (½ tsp) tumeric

5 ml (1 tsp) grated ginger
2 ml (¼ tsp) black pepper
5 ml (1 tsp) paprika

juice of 1 orange	grated rind of 1 orange
2 cloves garlic, pressed	285 ml (½ pint/1⅓ cups) water
2 medium onions, diced	565 g (1¼ lb/2½ cups) cubed
10 ml (1 dsp) cornflour (cornstarch)	lean lamb

1 Combine the liquids and flavourings in a casserole dish until smooth and well mixed.
2 Add the cubes of lamb and the onions and mix again.
3 Cook in the centre of the oven at 400°C/200°C/gas mark 6 for approximately 1½ hours or until the meat is tender.
4 Mix the cornflour (cornstarch) with a little water and stir into the casserole. Bring to the boil and simmer for 2 minutes.

LAMB KEBABS (SERVES 4)

Serve with plain rice or Nut Pilau (see *Lamb with Nut Pilau, page 131)* and salads.

1 clove garlic, pressed	15 ml (1 tbsp) lemon juice
15 ml (1 tbsp) tomato purée	30 ml (2 tbsp) olive oil
3 ml (½ tsp) ground ginger	2 ml (¼ tsp) black pepper
5 ml (1 tsp) paprika	565 g (1¼ lb/2½ cups) lean lamb
8 medium mushrooms	1 onion
or 1 large pepper	

1 Mix all the ingredients except the lamb and vegetables to form a marinade. Cube the lamb and toss in the marinade. Leave to stand for at least 2 hours.
2 Cut the onion into quarters and separate each quarter into its layers (a large piece of onion will not cook in the time it takes to cook the meat). If using the pepper, cut into eight pieces.
3 Thread the meat, mushrooms or pepper and the onion layers onto 4 large skewers. Brush the vegetables with the marinade.
4 Place on a baking tray and bake at 400°C/200°C/gas mark 6 for 30 minutes, turning once during cooking.

LAMB KORMA WITH BANANAS (SERVES 4)

Serve with brown rice, millet or quinoa and with curry accompaniments, salads or vegetables.

If allowed, stir 140 ml (¼ pint/½ cup) yogurt gradually into the korma just before serving.

5 onions

5 ml (1 tsp) ground coriander

3 ml (½ tsp)ground cardamom

2 ml (¼ tsp) cinnamon

2 ml (¼ tsp) black pepper

2 cloves garlic, pressed

10 ml (1 dsp) tomato purée (optional)

425 ml (¾ pint/2 cups) boiling water

565 g (1¼ lb/2½ cups) lean lamb, cubed

2 bananas

15 ml (1 tbsp) olive oil

3 ml (½ tsp) ground cumin

2 ml (¼ tsp) ground cloves

3 ml (½ tsp) tumeric

5 ml (1 tsp) garam masala

5 ml (1 tsp) grated ginger

55 g (2 oz/⅓ cup) creamed coconut

20 ml (1 rounded tbsp) raisins (optional)

1 Finely slice 3 onions and sweat in the olive oil over a gentle heat, stirring regularly, until they are soft and golden brown. This will take approximately 30 minutes.

2 Add the spices and the garlic, and sweat for another few minutes.

3 Place the onion mixture, the ginger and the tomato purée in a food processor and blend until very smooth.

4 In a large casserole dish, dissolve the creamed coconut in the boiling water. Add the onion mixture and the meat and mix well.

5 Roughly chop the two remaining onions and add to the casserole dish, along with the raisins.

6 Place the casserole in the oven at 400°C/200°C/gas mark 6, and cook for 1½ hours or until the meat is tender.

7 Cut the bananas into 2-cm (½-in) lengths, and add to the casserole just before serving. They only need a few minutes to warm through.

CHICKEN KORMA WITH GREEN PEPPER (SERVES 4)

Follow the previous recipe, substituting chicken for the lamb, green pepper for the bananas, and use a large tin of chopped tomatoes in tomato juice instead of 285 ml (½ pint/1⅓ cups) of water. Slice the green pepper and add along with the other ingredients.

LAMB WITH NUT PILAU (SERVES 4)

Accompany with a salad or fresh vegetables.

225 g (8 oz/1 ⅙ cups) brown rice	1 medium onion
2 cloves garlic	10 ml (1 dsp) olive oil
2 ml (¼ tsp) ground cardamom	5 ml (1 tsp) ground cumin
5 ml (1 tsp) ground coriander	1 ml (⅛ tsp) chilli powder
2 ml (¼ tsp) tumeric	3 ml (½ tsp) cinnamon
710 ml (1¼ pints/3 ⅛ cups) good stock	30 g (1 oz/⅕ cup) raisins (optional)
55g (2 oz/½ cup) toasted split almonds	4 lamb chops

1 Soak the rice in lots of warm water for 20 minutes. Rinse and drain.
2 Finely chop the onion and press the garlic clove. Sweat the onion and garlic in the olive oil until they begin to soften and brown.
3 Add the rice and the spices, and sweat for another few minutes.
4 Add the stock and the raisins, bring to the boil, cover and simmer for approximately 40–50 minutes until the rice is cooked and all the liquid has been absorbed. To prevent the rice becoming too dry it may be necessary to add a little more water during cooking, especially towards the end.
5 Grill the chops while the rice is cooking.
6 Finally, toss the almonds into the rice, and serve with the chops on top.

Fish Dishes

COD PROVENÇALE (SERVES 4)

This fish dish is quick and easy to make yet delicious enough for entertaining. Try salmon or monkfish instead of the cod or add prawns or mussels. If you cannot tolerate tomatoes, try using carrot juice.

3 ml (½ tsp) dried oregano
2 ml (¼ tsp) dried thyme
1 bay leaf
140 ml (5 fl oz/⅔ cup) water
1 onion, chopped
1 green pepper, diced
455 g (1 lb/2 cups) cod (thick piece), cut or flaked into bite-sized pieces

3 ml (½ tsp) dried basil
5 ml (1 tsp) fennel seeds
black pepper
570 ml (1 pint/2½ cups) creamed tomatoes or tomato juice
1 clove garlic, pressed
parsley to garnish

1 Place the herbs, seasoning, water, tomatoes, vegetables and garlic in a pan and cook for 10 minutes.
2 Add the fish to the tomato mixture and cook gently for 5 minutes or until the fish is just cooked. Do not stir roughly or the fish will break up.
3 Serve on rice, sprinkled with lots of fresh parsley.

MACKEREL IN GINGER AND ORANGE (SERVES 4)

juice of 2 oranges
5 ml (1 tsp) grated ginger
black pepper

grated rind of 1 orange
10 ml (1 dsp) tomato purée
4 mackerel fillets

1 Mix together the orange juice, rind, ginger, tomato purée and black pepper.

2 Marinate the mackerel fillets in the mixture for at least 3 hours.
3 Bake in a covered container in the marinade at 400°F/200°C/
gas mark 6 for 20–25 minutes or until the fish is just cooked.
Serve hot or cold with the juices poured over the fish.

FISH FLORENTINE (SERVES 4)

You could bake the fish pieces together in a larger gratin dish, but
extend the cooking time to approximately 20–25 minutes. A little
grated cheese mixed with breadcrumbs could be used instead of
the ground nuts, if allowed.

455 g (1 lb/8 cups) spinach
425 ml (¾ pint/2 cups) White Sauce
   (see Chapter 8, page 145)

4 pieces fish e.g. cod, haddock,
   salmon
20 ml (2 dsp) ground nuts

1 Wash the spinach and lightly cook in the water in which it has
been washed for 3–5 minutes.
2 Drain the spinach and divide between four individual gratin
dishes.
3 Lay a piece of fish on each spinach bed.
4 Make the white sauce as directed and pour evenly over the fish.
Sprinkle the nuts over the surface.
5 Bake for approximately 15 minutes near the top of the oven at
400°F/200°C/gas mark 6 until the top is lightly brown and the
fish is just cooked.

STIR-FRY WITH PRAWNS AND PEACHES (SERVES 4)

If allowed, add 15 ml (1 tbsp) of shoyu/tamari sauce for extra flavour. Note that prawns do contain salt unless freshly shelled.

1 bunch spring onions (scallions)
2 medium peaches
455 g (1 lb/2¾ cups) cooked rice
115 g (4 oz/1 cup) prawns
black pepper

2 carrots
10 ml (1 dsp) olive oil
30 ml (2 tbsp) water
115 g (4 oz/1 cup) toasted cashews

1 Finely slice the spring onions (scallions), cut the carrots into matchstick pieces and dice the peaches.
2 Sweat the carrots and spring onions (scallions) in the olive oil until just beginning to soften.
3 Add the remaining ingredients and sweat until warmed through.

PEPPERED COD (SERVES 4)

Serve with crisp stir-fried vegetables, rice and salad. Green peppercorns are available bottled in brine. You could, however, use dried green or black peppercorns soaked overnight in a little boiling water, or even coarsley ground black pepper. Use dried herbs if you do not have fresh or frozen. Line the grill pan with foil to make washing-up easier.

10 ml (1 dsp) fresh chopped herbs ·
    e.g. parsley, tarragon, dill, fennel
15 ml (1 tbsp) lemon juice
3 ml (½ tsp) paprika

5 ml (1 tsp) green peppercorns
30 ml (2 tbsp) olive oil
4 cod fillets

1 Finely chop the peppercorns and mix along with the herbs in the oil and lemon juice.
2 Spread the mixture evenly over the cod fillets and sprinkle with the paprika.

3 Cook under a hot grill with the rack removed from the grillpan for approximately 10 minutes or until the fish is browning and just cooked. Do not turn over.

GRILLED FISH WITH TOMATO AND PESTO (SERVES 4)

It is best to use homemade pesto sauce as the bought varieties usually contain cheese. Line the grillpan with foil to save on washing-up.

40 ml (4 dsp) olive oil	40 ml (4 dsp) lemon juice
1 clove garlic, pressed	4 pieces of fish
4 large tomatoes	10 ml (1 dsp) pesto sauce (see
black pepper	Chapter 8, page 146)

1 Mix the oil, lemon juice and garlic. Pour over the fish and allow to marinade for at least 10 minutes.
2 Skin and finely dice the tomatoes, and mix with the pesto sauce and the pepper.
3 Cook the fish under a hot grill with the rack removed from the grill pan for approximately 10 minutes or until the fish is just cooked. Baste with the marinade during cooking.
4 Serve with the tomato and pesto mixture spread over the top of the fish.

FRIED FISH (SERVES 4)

The cornmeal gives the fish a lovely golden colour but you can use soya or rice flour if you cannot tolerate corn.

40 ml (4 dsp) cornmeal	black pepper
4 pieces filleted fish	30 ml (2 tbsp) olive oil

1 Mix the cornmeal and pepper on a plate.
2 Wash the fish, dry a little with kitchen roll then dip into the cornmeal until the fish is well coated on both sides.

3 Fry the fish in the olive oil until it is golden brown on both sides and cooked through.

FISH PARCELS (SERVES 4)

Serve on rice, millet or quinoa accompanied by salad or cooked vegetables.

4 pieces fish (preferably thick)	1 leek or 4 spring onions (scallions)
1 stick (stalk) celery	1 carrot
1 small courgette (zucchini)	15 ml (1 tbsp) chopped parsley
1 large tomato	5 ml (1 tsp) grated orange rind
juice of 1 orange	10 ml (1 dsp) lemon juice
5 ml (1 tsp) grated ginger	black pepper

1 Place each piece of fish on a piece of foil approximately 25-cm (10-in) square.
2 Slice the leek or spring onions (scallions) into ½-cm (⅛-in) pieces.
3 Cut the celery and carrot into very fine matchstick pieces.
4 Thinly slice the courgette (zucchini).
5 Sprinkle the vegetables on top of the fish, along with the parsley.
6 Skin and finely dice the tomato and mix with the remaining ingredients. Pour over the fish and vegetables.
7 Lift the corners of the foil and twist to form parcels.
8 Place on a baking tray and bake at 400°F/200°C/gas mark 6 for approximately 15–20 minutes or until the fish is just cooked.

FISH PIE (SERVES 4)

If allowed, add a knob of butter to the mashed potatoes. If you cannot tolerate potatoes, try topping the fish pie with a mixture of mashed parsnip and cooked millet. Prawns do contain salt unless freshly cooked and shelled, but another fish or vegetable could be used instead.

900 g (2 lb/6½ cups) potatoes
455 g (1 lb/2 cups) cod or haddock
55 g (2 oz/⅓ cup) fresh or frozen peas
olive oil

black pepper
115 g (4 oz/1 cup) prawns
55 g (2 oz/¼ cup) sweetcorn
kernels

White sauce
30 ml (2 level tbsp) cornflour (cornstarch)
285 ml (½ pt/1 ⅓ cups) soya
   or almond milk
2 ml (¼ tsp) nutmeg
3 ml (½ tsp) grated lemon rind
black pepper

3 ml (½ tsp) mustard
140 ml (¼ pt/⅔ cup) potato
   cooking water
5 ml (1 tsp) lemon juice
15 ml (1 tbsp) chopped parsley

1 Peel and chop the potatoes and boil in water until soft. Mash using a little of the cooking liquid to give a soft consistency, and season with black pepper. Save the remaining cooking liquid to use in the white sauce.
2 To make the white sauce, mix the cornflour (cornstarch) and mustard with a little milk in a saucepan. Add the rest of the milk, 140 ml (¼ pint/⅔ cup) of potato water and the remaining sauce ingredients. Bring to the boil, stirring constantly, then lower the heat and simmer for 2 minutes.
3 Cut the fish into small pieces and add to the sauce along with the prawns, peas and sweetcorn, and mix gently.
4 Place the fish mixture into a gratin dish and spread the mashed potato over the top.
5 Brush the surface with olive oil and bake near the top of the oven at 400°F/200°C/gas mark 6 for 30 minutes. If the surface is not brown enough, place under a hot grill for a few minutes.

SEAFOOD PASTA (SERVES 4)

Follow the previous recipe, but instead of topping with mashed potatoes, mix the fish sauce with cooked pasta. Use 225 g (8 oz/2½ cups) pasta, made from rice, corn or buckwheat.

FISH WITH RED ONIONS AND GREEN PEPPERS (SERVES 4)

Serve with baked potatoes and a salad. The fish pieces could be baked together in a large gratin dish, but allow an extra 5 minutes cooking time.

4 red onions	2 green peppers
4 thick pieces of fish (e.g. cod, haddock)	45 ml (3 tbsp) olive oil
30 ml (2 tbsp) lemon juice	black pepper

1 Slice the onions into rings and the green peppers into strips.
2 Sweat the onions and peppers in 15 ml (1 tbsp) olive oil until they begin to soften and brown. This will take approximately 20 minutes. Stir frequently and do not be tempted to turn the heat up too high.
3 Divide the onion and pepper mixture between 4 small gratin dishes and place a piece of fish on top of the vegetables.
4 Mix the remaining 30 ml (2 tbsp) olive oil with the lemon juice and spread over the fish. Sprinkle with lots of black pepper.
5 Cover with foil and bake at 400°F/200°C/gas mark 6 for approximately 15 minutes or until the fish is just cooked.

TUNA AND LENTIL BAKE (SERVES 4)

The surface could be sprinkled with grated cheese, if allowed.

170 g (6 oz/1 cup) red split lentils	1 large onion, diced
10 ml (1 dsp) olive oil	2 large eggs
140 ml (¼ pint/⅔ cup) soya or almond milk	200 g (7 oz/1 ⅓ cups) tuna in water
black pepper	30 ml (2 tbsp) chopped nuts

1 Wash the lentils and bring to the boil in a pan with 570 ml (1 pint/ 2½ cups) of water. Simmer for 20–25 minutes until the lentils are soft and most of the liquid has been absorbed.
2 Sweat the onion in the oil until it begins to soften.

3 Separate the eggs and beat the yolks and milk together. Whisk the egg whites until stiff.
4 Flake the tuna fish and include the juices from the tin.
5 Combine the lentils, onion, tuna, egg, milk and pepper. Fold in the egg whites using a metal spoon.
6 Pour the mixture into a shallow, greased ovenproof dish, sprinkle the surface with the nuts and bake at 350°F/180°C/gas mark 4 for 30 minutes or until the bake is set and brown.

KEDGEREE (SERVES 4)

225 g (8 oz/1⅙ cups) brown rice
10 ml (1 dsp) olive oil
225 g (8 oz/1 cup) fresh fish
15 ml (1 tbsp) fresh parsley

2 large onions, diced
2 hardboiled eggs (optional)
55 g (2 oz/½ cup) prawns

Sauce
30 ml (2 tbsp) fish cooking liquid
30 ml (2 tbsp) olive oil
15 ml (1 tbsp) lemon juice
3 ml (½ tsp) grated lemon rind

5 ml (1 tsp) curry powder
80 ml (4 tbsp) mayonnaise or
    soya yogurt

1 Cook the brown rice, sieve and keep warm.
2 Sweat the onions in the oil until they begin to soften and brown. Cut the eggs into rough dice.
3 In a pan poach the fish in 30 ml (2 tbsp) water until just cooked. Flake the fish and remove any skin or bones.
4 Mix the rice, fish, prawns, eggs, onions and parsley.
5 Make the sauce by blending 30 ml (2 tbsp) of the fish liquid with the curry powder and the oil. It is best to use a food processor, if available, in order to obtain a thick emulsion. Add the mayonnaise or yogurt and the lemon juice and rind.
6 Pour the sauce over the fish and rice and mix gently with a fork.

FISH CAKES (SERVES 4)

Substitute butter beans if you cannot eat eggs.

565 g (1¼ lb/4 cups) potatoes
1 large onion
2 hardboiled eggs
20 ml (2 dsp) lemon juice
olive oil

1 tin (400 g/14 oz/2 cups) tuna
  fish (in water)
30 ml (2 tbsp) chopped parsley
black pepper

1 Cook the potatoes in boiling water until soft. Mash using the drained water from the tuna to give a soft consistency.
2 Finely dice the onion and cook in 30 ml (2 tbsp) of water until soft. Sieve to remove the water.
3 Chop the hardboiled egg and stir into the potatoes along with the onion, tuna, parsley, lemon juice and black pepper.
4 Shape into 12 cakes and place on a well-greased baking tray. Brush the fish cakes with olive oil, and cook on the top shelf of a hot oven at 450°F/230°C/gas mark 8 for approximately 20 minutes or until brown.

TUNA, BUTTER BEAN AND LEEK SAVOURY (SERVES 4)

455 g (1 lb/4 cups) leeks
140 ml (¼ pint/⅔ cup) water
285 ml (½ pint/1⅓ cups) soya
  or almond milk
2 ml (¼ tsp) ground nutmeg
3 ml (½ tsp) grated lemon rind
black pepper
15 ml (1 tbsp) chopped nuts

1 large carrot
200 g (7 oz/1⅓ cups) tinned
  tuna in water
30 ml (2 level tbsp) cornflour
  (cornstarch)
10 ml (1 dsp) fresh parsley
225 g (8 oz/1 cup) cooked butter
  beans

1 Slice the leeks and cut the carrot into matchstick pieces. Cook in 140 ml (¼ pint/⅔ cup) of water, sieve and save the cooking liquid.
2 Drain and flake the tuna fish, saving the juices from the tin.

3 Make the milk up to 425 ml (¾ pint/2 cups) with the tuna and vegetable liquids. Add a little water if necessary.
4 Mix the milk and cornflour (cornstarch) together in a pan until smooth. Bring to the boil, stirring constantly, and simmer for 2 minutes.
5 Mix all the ingredients except the nuts into the sauce, taking care when mixing the butter beans so that they do not break up.
6 Place the mixture into 1 large or 4 small gratin dishes. Sprinkle the surface with nuts and serve.

QUICK FISH CASSEROLE (SERVES 4)

Serve with rice, millet or quinoa and salad or vegetables.

1 carrot	½ onion
4 portions fish (e.g. cod, haddock, hake)	10 ml (1 dsp) olive oil
140 ml (¼ pint/⅔ cup) water	1 bay leaf
10 ml (1 dsp) cornflour (cornstarch)	black pepper
140 ml (¼ pint/⅔ cup) soya or almond milk	80 ml (4 tbsp) frozen peas

1 Grate the carrot and onion and sweat in the olive oil for 3 minutes.
2 Add the fish and turn to coat with the vegetables and oil. Add the water, the bay leaf and some black pepper. Cover the pan and cook gently until the fish is almost cooked, approximately 10 minutes.
3 Mix the cornflour (cornstarch) and milk to a smooth paste and add to the pan, mixing with the juices and vegetables. Bring to the boil, add the frozen peas, cover and cook gently for another 5 minutes.

MAJORCAN FISH CASSEROLE (SERVES 4)

680 g (1½ lb/5 cups) potatoes
(even sized)
1 courgette (zucchini)
225 g (½ lb/4 cups) spinach
30 ml (2 tbsp) raisins (optional)
2 ml (¼ tsp) dried thyme
2 ml (¼ tsp) dried marjoram
3 ml (½ tsp) fennel seeds
4 pieces cod or hake

1 large onion
10 ml (1 dsp) olive oil
30 ml (2 tbsp) pine nuts
1 tin (400 g/15 oz/2 cups)
chopped tomatoes in tomato
juice
black pepper
olive oil for brushing the surface

1 Boil the potatoes whole in their skins for approximately 10–15 minutes, depending on the size of the potatoes. They should be slightly undercooked at this stage. Allow to cool.
2 Dice the onion and sweat in the olive oil until it begins to soften and brown. Dice the courgette (zucchini), add to the pan and sweat the vegetables for a few more minutes.
3 Chop the spinach and add to the onion and courgette (zucchini) along with the pine nuts, raisins, tomatoes, herbs and pepper. Bring to the boil and simmer for 5 minutes.
4 Place the mixture into 1 large or 4 small gratin dishes. Lay the fish pieces on top.
5 Skin the potatoes then grate them using a food processor or hand grater. Pile the grated potatoes on top of the fish, pressing down a little but leaving the surface rough.
6 Brush the surface with olive oil and bake at the top of the oven for approximately 15 minutes for the small dishes and 20 minutes for the larger at 400°F/200°C/gas mark 6. Place under a hot grill for 2 minutes if the potatoes have not browned sufficiently in the oven.

Sauces and Dressings

FRENCH DRESSING

If allowed, 5 ml (1 tsp) of honey makes this dressing taste less sharp. If you do not like the taste of olive oil, use half sunflower oil, but gradually keep reducing the amount as you become accustomed to the taste of olive oil. If you cannot tolerate citrus fruits but can tolerate cider vinegar, use one-third vinegar and two-thirds olive oil.

juice of 1 orange
olive oil
black pepper
3 ml (½ tsp) orange rind

juice of 1 lemon
10 ml (1 dsp) mustard
3 ml (½ tsp) lemon rind

Choose 4 dried herbs from the following:
- 3 ml (½ tsp) parsley
- 3 ml (½ tsp) dill seeds
- 3 ml (½ tsp) celery seeds
- 3 ml (½ tsp) mint
- 3 ml (½ tsp) chives
- 3 ml (½ tsp) fennel seeds
- 3 ml (½ tsp) tarragon

If substituting fresh herbs, use 5 ml (1 tsp) of each.

Other flavourings which could be added include:
- 3 ml (½ tsp) paprika
- 5 ml (1 tsp) tahini
- 5 ml (1 tsp) grated raw onion
- 5 ml (1 tsp) tomato purée
- 3 ml (½ tsp) grated ginger
- 1 clove garlic, pressed

1 Place the orange and lemon juice in a screw-topped jar and add an equal amount of olive oil.
2 Add the remaining ingredients and shake well.
3 Store in the fridge ready for use.

TOFU MAYONNAISE

Flavour with garlic, curry powder, tomato purée, spring onion (scallion) or herbs, if desired.

1 packet (290 g/10 oz/1 cup) silken tofu
170 ml (6 fl oz/¾ cup) oil (use a mixture of olive oil and sunflower)

15 ml (1 tbsp) lemon juice
5 ml (1 tsp) mustard
black pepper

1 Process the tofu, lemon juice, mustard and pepper in a food processor.
2 Slowly add the oils through the funnel of the food processor with the machine on full power.
3 Store the mayonnaise in a covered container in the fridge.

MAYONNAISE

The amount of oil varies according to the size of the eggs. I never measure the oil but just pour it from the bottle until the mayonnaise is the right thickness. Olive oil can be used on its own, but this produces quite a strong-flavoured mayonnaise.

Vary the mayonnaise by adding flavourings such as herbs, garlic, curry powder, tomato purée or spring onions (scallions).

15 ml (1 tbsp) lemon juice
2 egg yolks + 30 ml (2 tbsp) water or 1 whole egg
black pepper

10 ml (l dsp) mustard
approximately 170 ml (6 fl oz/¾ cup) oil (use a mixture of olive and sunflower)

1 Process all the ingredients except the oil in a food processor until well mixed.
2 Leave the food processor running on high power and *very* slowly add the oil a few drops at a time until it starts to emulsify. Then add the rest of the oil slowly until the desired thickness of mayonnaise is obtained.
3 Store in the fridge and use as required.

THOUSAND ISLAND MAYONNAISE

Add the following ingredients to the previous recipe for Mayonnaise and mix:

10 ml (1 dsp) finely chopped parsley
10 ml (1 dsp) finely chopped onions or chives
10 ml (1 dsp) tomato purée

30 ml (2 tbsp) chopped green olives
30 ml (2 tbsp) finely chopped green pepper

WHITE SAUCE

30 ml (2 level tbsp) cornflour (cornstarch)
3 ml (½ tsp) lemon rind
2 ml (¼ tsp) nutmeg
black pepper

5 ml (1 level tsp) mustard
425 ml (¾ pt/2 cups) soya, rice or almond milk
1 bay leaf

1 In a saucepan, mix the cornflour (cornstarch), mustard and a little milk together until smooth.
2 Add the remaining milk along with the lemon rind, nutmeg, bay leaf and black pepper.
3 Bring to the boil, stirring constantly. Simmer for 2 minutes.
4 Remove the bay leaf.

PARSLEY SAUCE

Add 30 ml (2 tbsp) of finely chopped parsley to the previous recipe for White Sauce.

ONION SAUCE

Boil a finely diced onion in 140 ml (¼ pint/⅔ cup) of water until soft. Drain, keep the liquid and use this instead of some of the milk in the recipe for White Sauce *(see above)*. Add the onions to the cooked sauce along with lots of black pepper and the other ingredients.

MUSHROOM SAUCE

Add 115 g (4 oz/1 cup) sliced and sautéed mushrooms to the White Sauce *(see page 145)*.

VELOUTÉ SAUCE

Use a good quality stock instead of half of the milk in the recipe for White Sauce *(see page 145)*.

PESTO SAUCE

55 g (2 oz/2 cups) fresh basil leaves   30 g (1 oz/¼ cup) pine nuts
1 clove garlic   black pepper
60 ml (2 fl oz/¼ cup) olive oil

1 Using a pestle and mortar or food processor, blend the basil, pine nuts, garlic and black pepper thoroughly, then gradually work in the olive oil to give a smooth mixture.
2 Store in the fridge.

HERB AND WALNUT SAUCE

Substitute walnuts for the pine nuts in the previous recipe for Pesto Sauce, and a selection of herbs such as parsley, mint, chives, tarragon, coriander and dill instead of the basil leaves.

Serve 5 ml (1 tsp) mixed into a bowl of freshly boiled rice for a delicious snack. Pesto Sauce and Herb and Walnut Sauce can also be used to add flavour to risottos, soups and casseroles.

RATATOUILLE SAUCE

Serve as a sauce or vegetable accompaniment.

½ aubergine (eggplant)
½ red pepper
1 large onion
570 ml (½ pint/2½ cups) water
3 ml (½ tsp) dried basil
3 ml (½ tsp) dried oregano

½ green pepper
2 courgettes (zucchini)
1 large tin (400 g/15 oz/2 cups)
   chopped tomatoes in tomato
   juice

1 Dice the aubergine (eggplant) and peppers and slice the courgettes (zucchini) and onion.
2 Place all the ingredients into a saucepan and bring to the boil.
3 Cover the pan and simmer for 40 minutes.

FRESH TOMATO SAUCE

A large tin (400 g/15 oz/2 cups) of chopped tomatoes could be
substituted for the fresh ones.

455 g (1 lb/2½ cups) fresh tomatoes
30ml (2 tbsp) chopped fresh herbs
   e.g. parsley, chives, basil, coriander,
   marjoram or 5 ml (1 tsp) dried
   herbs e.g. basil, oregano

½ small onion
1 clove garlic
10 ml (1 dsp) olive oil
3 ml (½ tsp) paprika
black pepper

1 Finely dice the onion and press the garlic clove. Place the oil in
   a saucepan and sweat the garlic and onion for a few minutes
   until soft and beginning to brown.
2 Skin and chop the tomatoes and add to the pan.
3 Add the remaining ingredients and cook until the tomatoes
   have just melted, no more than 5 minutes.
4 Serve immediately with nut roasts, vegetables, rice etc.

VEGETABLE PURÉE SAUCE

Serve with nut roasts, rice, fish or chicken. Fresh herbs could be added if desired, such as parsley, chives, basil, coriander, marjoram.

1 medium onion	4 large carrots
2 large tomatoes	285 ml (½ pint/1⅓ cups) water
5 ml (1 tsp) lemon juice	black pepper

1 Dice the onion and slice the carrots. Skin the tomatoes.
2 Cook the onion and carrot in the water until they are just soft, then allow to cool slightly.
3 Process the carrot, onion and water in a food processor until smooth. Add the tomatoes, lemon juice and pepper and process again.
4 Heat through but do not cook further.

DAHL

Use as a sauce for vegetarian roasts, or on its own with brown rice or Spicy Baked Chicken (see Chapter 6, page 126). If allowed, 30 ml (2 tbsp) of yogurt can be added just before serving.

A variation on the above can be made by substituting whole green lentils for the red lentils and adding a finely diced onion. This dish is ideal to serve along with a meat dish and a vegetarian dish as part of an Indian-style meal.

200 g (7 oz/1 cup) red split lentils	1 clove garlic
3 ml (½ tsp) ground coriander	3 ml (½ tsp) tumeric
5 ml (1 tsp) cumin seeds	2 ml (¼ tsp) cayenne pepper
3 ml (½ tsp) garam masala	5 ml (1 tsp) grated ginger
990 ml (1¾ pints/4½ cups) water	

1 Wash the lentils, press the garlic clove and place all the ingredients in a saucepan. Bring to the boil.
2 Simmer gently, stirring occasionally, for 1½ hours.

CURRY SAUCE

Serve as a sauce to add flavour to rice, meat or vegetables. A vegetable curry can be made by adding 455 g (1 lb/3–4 cups) of chopped mixed vegetables and cooking in the sauce until tender. Alternatively, make an egg curry by hardboiling one egg per person and serving the egg halved, on top of rice, with the sauce poured over.

1 large onion	1 large baking apple
10 ml (1 dsp) olive oil	5 ml (1 tsp) curry powder
850 ml (1½ pints/3¾ cups) water	55 g (2 oz/⅓ cup) red split lentils
30 g (1 oz/⅙ cup) creamed coconut	30 ml (2 tbsp) raisins (optional)
15 ml (1 tbsp) tomato purée (optional)	

1 Dice the onion and grate the baking apple. Sweat the onion in the oil until it begins to soften and brown.
2 Add the grated apple and the curry powder and sweat for a few more minutes.
3 Add the remaining ingredients, bring to the boil and simmer, covered, for at least 1 hour until the lentils and apples have become part of a thick sauce. Stir occasionally during cooking and add a little more water if the sauce is too dry.

CHICKPEA AND AVOCADO SAUCE

Use as a sauce with rice, nut roasts, vegetables etc. or as a dip with vegetable crudités. Add more water if a softer sauce is required.

1 medium avocado	15 ml (1 tbsp) lemon juice
45 ml (3 tbsp) water	15 ml (1 tbsp) olive oil
115 g (4 oz/⅔ cup) cooked chickpeas	15 ml (1 tbsp) tahini

1 Process the avocado with the lemon juice, water and olive oil in a food processor.
2 Add the tahini and chickpeas and process until a smooth sauce is obtained.

FENNEL AND CASHEW NUT SAUCE

Serve with rice, millet, quinoa or pasta.

225 g (8 oz/2 cups) leeks
140 ml (5 fl oz/²/₃ cup) water or stock
3 ml (½ tsp) grated ginger
30 ml (1 oz/¼ cup) cashew nuts

225 g (8 oz/2 cups) fennel
3 ml (½ tsp) fennel seeds
black pepper
140 ml (5 fl oz/²/₃ cup) soya or
    almond milk

1 Slice the leeks, using mainly the white stems, and dice the fennel.
2 Bring to the boil in the water or stock, add the fennel seeds, the ginger and the pepper and simmer for 10 minutes.
3 In a food processor, process the cashew nuts until fine, then add the leek and fennel mixture and process again until the sauce is smooth and creamy.
4 Return to the pan along with the milk, bring the sauce to the boil and serve.

PEA AND CARAWAY SAUCE

170 g (6 oz/¾ cup) dried
    marrowfat peas
black pepper

200 ml (7 fl oz/¾ cup) water
5 ml (1 tsp) caraway seeds

1 Soak the peas overnight in lots of water. Rinse the peas, cover with boiling water, bring to the boil and cook until soft (this will only take approximately 10 minutes in a pressure cooker).
2 Drain off the excess liquid. Using this liquid and some extra water if necessary, measure out 200 ml (7 fl oz/¾ cup) and add this to the peas along with the pepper and caraway seeds.
3 Bring to the boil and simmer until the peas fall to form a sauce. Add a little more water if needed.

Baking Without

Because the baked goods in this section contain very little fat and no sugar, they will not keep for long. Store in the fridge and eat within three days. They may be cut into slices, or packed in small portions and stored in the freezer to be used as needed. If you cannot tolerate eggs, you will find a variety of egg replacers available in health-food shops, or make your own by following the recipe in the Introduction *(see page 42)*. Egg replacers will help to bind ingredients together but do not help mixtures to rise as do ordinary eggs. It may be necessary to add an extra 3 ml (½ tsp) baking powder in cakes and breads where a light texture is desired.

Potassium baking powder is also available in health-food shops, and is used in place of ordinary baking powder in these recipes to avoid the use of excess sodium. If you cannot find either potassium baking powder or egg replacer in your local health-food shop then do ask as these are available from the wholesalers but may not have been requested before.

I have tried to use the more readily available flours, but others could be substituted. The range is continually increasing. Do experiment with other flours if you cannot use the ones suggested. Also try using alternative flours instead of wheat flour in some of your favourite recipes. For 170 g (6 oz/1¼ cups) of wheat flour, substitute 115 g (4 oz/⅔ cup) cornmeal, 85 g (3 oz/½ cup) potato flour, 140 g (5 oz/¾ cup) rice flour or 85 g (3 oz/1 cup) soya flour.

It is difficult to make cakes without some form of sweetening, and so dried fruit has been used in quite a few of these recipes. I find that many individuals with *Candida albicans* can tolerate dried fruit if used sparingly, but some who have an intolerance or allergy to yeast will not be able to use any. These individuals could try using crystallized ginger and pineapple or dried apple to obtain some sweetness. Although the ginger and pineapple contain some sugar, they do not contain yeast, and it is probably better to use these than to abandon *Cooking Without* and end up eating a bar of chocolate in desperation for something sweet.

If possible, use scales to measure the ingredients for the following recipes as cup measurements may not be accurate enough to obtain good results. Similarly, it is best to use measuring spoons rather than the spoons in the cutlery drawer as these do vary a lot in size.

FRUIT AND NUT SLICES

If you do not have a food processor, grate the carrot and apple finely and chop the nuts, then mix all the ingredients together. This produces a slice which is more chunky and chewy. These slices benefit from the rice being well cooked and are ideal to make with an overcooked batch. Cooked millet or quinoa can be used instead of rice. A baking or an eating apple can be used.

1 large carrot
115 g (4 oz/^{2}/$_3$ cup) rice flour
3 ml (^{1}/$_2$ tsp) cinnamon
225 g (8 oz/1 ^{1}/$_3$ cups) well-cooked brown rice
55 g (2 oz/^{1}/$_2$ cup) hazelnuts

1 large apple
90 ml (3 fl oz/^{1}/$_3$ cup) water
3 ml (^{1}/$_2$ tsp) nutmeg
2 eggs or egg replacer
55 g (2 oz/^{1}/$_2$ cup) raisins (optional)
sesame or sunflower seeds to decorate

1 Line a shallow tin (approximately 30 cm by 23cm or 12 in by 9 in) with greaseproof paper or foil and oil the surface.
2 Roughly chop the carrot and apple and place in a food processor with the rice flour, water, spices, cooked rice and eggs. Process until fairly smooth.
3 Add the fruit and nuts and process for approximately 10 seconds until the fruit and nuts are chopped a little but still in pieces.
4 Place the mixture into the prepared tin and smooth the surface. Mark into 16 sections and sprinkle the surface with sunflower or sesame seeds.
5 Bake at 400°F/200°C/gas mark 6 for 20 minutes.

6 Cool in the tin, then turn the slices over and peel off the paper or foil.

7 Store in an airtight container in the fridge and use within 3 days. Alternatively, pack in handy-sized portions and freeze ready for snacks to take to work or on outings.

PARSNIP, BANANA AND APRICOT SLICES

Use the previous recipe but substitute the carrot with a parsnip, the raisins with chopped dried apricots and add 55 g (2 oz/^{1}/$_3$ cup) banana to the mixture before processing.

CAROB SLICES

Carob slices, the Fruit and Nut Slices *(see page 152)* and the Savoury Slices *(see page 154)* are all based on the same recipe which was invented by a patient of mine whose young children were on this dietary regime. She wanted them to be able to take something to school for break time which seemed an acceptable snack food. I make batches twice weekly and keep them in the fridge. There is then always something to take to work, on outings or to nibble whenever a snack is needed.

1 large carrot
55 g (2 oz/^{1}/$_2$ cup) carob flour
90 ml (3 fl oz/^{1}/$_3$ cup) water
2 eggs or egg replacer
30 g (1 oz/^{1}/$_2$ cup) desiccated coconut
55 g (2 oz/^{1}/$_2$ cup) raisins (optional)
sunflower seeds to decorate

1 large apple
55 g (2 oz/^{1}/$_3$ cup) rice flour
225 g (8 oz/1 ^{1}/$_3$ cups) well-cooked brown rice
3 ml (^{1}/$_2$ tsp) mixed spice
55 g (2 oz/^{1}/$_2$ cup) hazelnuts

1 Line a shallow tin (approximately 30 cm by 23 cm or 12 in by 9 in) with greaseproof paper or foil and oil the surface.

2 Roughly chop the carrot and apple and place in a food processor along with the carob flour, rice flour, water, cooked rice, eggs and mixed spice. Process until well mixed and fairly smooth.

3 Add the coconut, raisins and hazelnuts and process for 10 seconds until the nuts and fruit are chopped a little but still in pieces.
4 Place the mixture in the prepared tin and smooth the surface. Mark into 16 sections and sprinkle the surface with sunflower seeds.
5 Bake at 400°F/200°C/gas mark 6 for 20 minutes.
6 Allow to cool in the tin, turn the slices over and peel off the paper or foil. Store in an airtight container in the fridge and use within 3 days or pack in small portions in the freezer.

SAVOURY SLICES

If the sun-dried tomatoes are not in olive oil, soak first in a little water to soften. Use a baking or an eating apple.

1 large carrot	1 large apple
115 g (4 oz/^{2}/$_3$ cup) rice flour	90 ml (3 fl oz/^{1}/$_3$ cup) water
5 ml (1 tsp) fennel seeds	3 ml (½ tsp) dried tarragon
2 ml (¼ tsp) chilli powder	225 g (8 oz/1 ^{1}/$_3$ cups) well-cooked
2 eggs or egg replacer	brown rice
30 g (1 oz/¼ cup) sunflower	55 g (2 oz/¼ cup) sweetcorn
or pumpkin seeds	kernels or frozen peas
4 sun-dried tomatoes	8 olives, quartered
sesame or poppy seeds to garnish	black pepper

1 Line a shallow tin (approximately 30 cm by 23 cm or 12 in by 9 in) with foil or greaseproof paper. Oil the surface.
2 Roughly chop the carrot and apple and place in a food processor with the rice flour, water, herbs and spices, the cooked brown rice and the eggs. Process until well mixed and fairly smooth.
3 Tip the mixture out into a bowl and mix in the sunflower or pumpkin seeds, the sweetcorn, the finely chopped sun-dried tomatoes and the olives.
4 Spread into the prepared tin and smooth the surface. Mark into 16 sections and sprinkle the surface with sesame or poppy seeds and lots of freshly ground black pepper.

5 Bake at 400°F/200°C/gas mark 6 for 20 minutes.
6 Allow to cool in the tin then turn the slices over and peel off the paper or foil. Store in an airtight container in the fridge and eat within 3 days or freeze and use as needed.

APPLE, DATE AND NUT MUFFINS

These muffins are delicious and a real treat for anyone who misses cakes. Do not, however, eat too many of them as they are high in fruit sugar. Individuals with *Candida* problems may need to resist these in the early stages of treatment.

The mixture can be cooked as a loaf by placing in a greased and lined loaf tin and baking for 1¼ hours at 350°F/180°C/gas mark 4. Remove from the tin, peel off the lining paper and cool on a wire tray.

225 g (8 oz/2 cups) cooking apples, weighed after peeling
55 g (2 oz/½ cup) chopped walnuts
2 ml (¼ tsp) nutmeg
20 ml (2 level dsp) potassium baking powder
240 ml (8 fl oz/1 cup) water

55 g (2 oz/½ cup) sultanas
55 g (2oz/½ cup) chopped dates
2 ml (¼ tsp) cinnamon
225 g (8 oz/1 ⅓ cups) rice flour
15 ml (1 tbsp) sunflower oil
1 egg or egg replacer

1 Cut the apple into 2-cm (½-in) dice and place in a bowl with the fruit and nuts.
2 Place the remaining ingredients in a food processor and process until smooth. If you do not have a food processor, beat together in a bowl.
3 Combine the two sets of ingredients.
4 Pile into 12 greased bun or muffin tins. The mixture will be piled up high if using bun tins but this will be fine.
5 Bake for approximately 20 minutes at 400°F/200°C/gas mark 6.
6 Remove from the tins and place on a wire tray to cool. Store in the fridge and eat within 3 days. The muffins can be frozen if desired.

BANANA, DATE AND NUT LOAF

Substitute 225 g (8 oz/2 cups) of chopped banana for the apple in the previous recipe.

GINGER AND ORANGE CAKE

If allowed, add crystallized ginger and candied peel instead of the sultanas for a really delicious but not too sinful cake. Individuals with *Candida albicans* may cope better with ginger than with dried fruit. If using an egg replacer, extra water may be needed to make the mixture into a soft consistency. Raw courgette (zucchini) can be used instead of the banana in this recipe.

115 g (4 oz/²/₃cup) potato flour
55 g (2 oz/²/₃ cup) ground almonds
55 g (2 oz/¹/₃ cup) banana
5 ml (1 tsp) grated orange rind
5 ml (1 tsp) ground ginger
1 egg or an egg replacer
85 g (3 oz/³/₄ cup) sultanas (optional)

55 g (2 oz/¹/₃ cup) rice flour
15 ml (1 tbsp) sunflower oil
juice of 1 orange made up to
170 ml (6 fl oz/³/₄ cup)
with water
20 ml (2 level dsp) potassium
baking powder

1 If a food processor is available, place all the ingredients except the sultanas into the goblet and process until smooth and well mixed. Alternatively, beat the egg in a bowl and add the remaining ingredients, beating well with a wooden spoon.
2 Add and mix in the sultanas.
3 Place the mixture in a small greased loaf tin and bake in the centre of the oven at 400°F/200°C/gas mark 6 for approximately 30 minutes or until golden brown and firm to the touch.
4 Turn out of the tin and cool on a wire tray. Keep in a covered container in the fridge and eat within 3 days.

CARROT AND COCONUT CAKE

If using an egg replacer, extra water may be needed to make the mixture into a soft consistency. Use grated courgette (zucchini) instead of the carrot if desired.

170 g (6 oz/1 cup) finely grated carrot
3 ml (½ tsp) nutmeg
3 ml (½ tsp) cinnamon
170 ml (6 fl oz/¾ cup) warm water
20 ml (2 level dsp) potassium
    baking powder
85 g (3 oz/¾ cup) sultanas (optional)

55 g (2 oz/⅔ cup) desiccated
    coconut
15 ml (1 tbsp) sunflower oil
140 g (5 oz/¾ cup) brown rice
    flour
1 egg or an egg replacer

1 If a processor is available, blend all the ingredients except the sultanas until smooth and well mixed. Alternatively, beat the egg in a bowl, add the other ingredients and beat well with a wooden spoon. Add and mix in the sultanas.
2 Place the mixture in a small greased loaf tin and bake in the centre of the oven at 400°F/200°C/gas mark 6 for approximately 40 minutes or until firm to the touch and golden brown. Cool on a wire tray.

POTATO FLOUR BREAD

If an egg replacer is used, extra water may be needed to make the mixture into a soft consistency.

115 g (4 oz/⅔ cup) potato flour
55 g (2 oz/⅔ cup) soya flour
15 ml (1 tbsp) sunflower oil
1 egg or an egg replacer

55 g (2 oz/⅓ cup) rice flour
170 ml (6 fl oz/¾ cup) warm water
20 ml (2 level dsp) potassium
    baking powder

1 If a food processor is available, place all the ingredients into the goblet and process until smooth and well mixed. Alternatively, beat the egg in a bowl and add the remaining ingredients, beating well with a wooden spoon.

2 Place in a small greased loaf tin and bake at 400°F/200°C/gas mark 6 for 30–35 minutes or until firm to the touch and golden brown.
3 Remove from the tin and cool on a wire tray. Store in an airtight container in the fridge and eat within 3 days.

CORNBREAD

If an egg replacer is used, extra water may be needed to make the mixture into a soft consistency.

115 g (4 oz/^{2}/$_3$ cup) medium maize meal
15 ml (1 tbsp) sunflower oil
1 egg or an egg replacer
½ small baking apple

55 g (2 oz/^{1}/$_3$ cup) potato flour
115 ml (4 fl oz/½ cup) warm water
20 ml (2 level dsp) potassium baking powder

1 Mix all the ingredients together in a food processor or, if mixing by hand, beat the egg and grate the apple, then beat in the remaining ingredients with a wooden spoon.
2 Place in a small greased loaf tin and bake at 400°F/200°C/gas mark 6 for 35 minutes.
3 Remove from the tin, cool on a wire tray and store in the fridge in an airtight container. Eat within 3 days.

ONION AND HERB LOAF

115 g (4 oz/^{2}/$_3$ cup) rice flour
55 g (2 oz/^{2}/$_3$ cup) soya flour
2 ml (¼ tsp) dried thyme
20 ml (2 level dsp) potassium baking powder
2 spring onions (scallions) or 15 ml (1 tbsp) minced onion
5 ml (1 level tsp) mustard

55 g (2 oz/^{1}/$_3$ cup) maize meal
5 ml (1 tsp) dried parsley
3 ml (½ tsp) dried sage
15 ml (1 tbsp) olive oil
310 ml (11 fl oz/1½ cups) warm water or 260 ml (9 fl oz/1¼ cups) warm water plus 1 egg

1 If using a food processor, place all the ingredients in the goblet and process until smooth and well mixed. If mixing by hand, place the mustard in a bowl and beat with a little water until smooth. Add the remaining ingredients and beat well with a wooden spoon.
2 Place the mixture in a small greased loaf tin and bake in the centre of the oven at 400°F/200°C/gas mark 6 for approximately 40 minutes until the loaf is brown and firm to the touch.
3 Remove from the tin and cool on a wire tray. Store in the fridge in an airtight container and eat within 3 days.

ONION AND HERB FOCACCIA BREAD

1 small onion
2 cloves garlic
30 ml (2 tbsp) fresh chopped herbs
    e.g. thyme, marjoram, parsley,
    rosemary, chives or 5 ml (1 tsp)
    dried herbs

15 ml (1 tbsp) olive oil
8 olives (optional)
3 sun-dried tomatoes
Onion and Herb Loaf mixture
    (see page 158)

1 Cut the onion in half and then into paper-thin slices. Place in a bowl and mix to coat with the olive oil.
2 Cut the garlic into very thin slices and the olives in half.
3 Cut the sun-dried tomatoes into small pieces.
4 Grease two baking trays. Make the Onion and Herb Loaf mixture and spread into 2 23-cm (9-in) rounds on the trays.
5 Spread the onion, garlic, olives, tomatoes and herbs over the surface and bake near the top of the oven at 400°F/200°C/gas mark 6 for 25–30 minutes until the bread is quite brown and crisp. Serve whilst still hot with salads or soup.

SPICED CARROT BREAD

If using an egg replacer, extra water may be needed to make the mixture into a soft consistency. Courgettes (zucchini) could be used to replace the carrot in this recipe.

140 g (5 oz/³⁄₄ cup) rice flour
  or millet flour
3 ml (¹⁄₂ tsp) nutmeg
90 ml (3 fl oz/¹⁄₃ cup) warm water
15 ml (1 tbsp) sunflower oil
1 egg or egg replacer

170 g (6 oz/1 cup) finely grated
  carrot
3 ml (¹⁄₂ tsp) cinnamon
20 ml (2 level dsp) potassium
  baking powder

1 If a food processor is available, place all the ingredients into the goblet and process until they are well mixed and smooth. Alternatively, beat the egg in a bowl and add the remaining ingredients, beating well with a wooden spoon.
2 Place the mixture in a small greased loaf tin and bake for approximately 35–40 minutes at 400°F/200°C/gas mark 6, or until firm to the touch and beginning to brown.
3 Turn out onto a wire tray to cool. Store in an airtight container in the fridge and eat within 3 days.

ALMOND AND SOYA BISCUITS

60 ml (4 level tbsp) carrot purée
45 g (1¹⁄₂ oz/¹⁄₂ cup) soya flour
115 g (4 oz/1 ¹⁄₃ cups) ground almonds
sunflower seeds to decorate

1 Cook a medium-sized carrot until tender. Purée in the food processor, then measure out 60 ml (4 tbsp).
2 Mix the carrot purée, soya flour and ground almonds in the food processor until you have a thick, sticky mixture.
3 Press together any loose pieces and roll out by hand into a sausage shape, approximately 3 cm (1 in) in diameter. Use a little soya flour if necessary to stop the mixture sticking.
4 Cut into thin slices, approximately ¹⁄₂ cm (¹⁄₈ in) thick using a sharp knife. There should be approximately 30 slices.
5 Lay the biscuits on a greased baking sheet. Press a few sunflower seeds into the surface of each biscuit.
6 Bake at 350°F/180°C/gas mark 4 for 20 minutes until beginning to brown and crisp around the edges.

7 Cool on a wire tray, then store in an airtight container and eat within 3 days.

CHEWY FRUIT BARS

This recipe may not be suitable for those with severe *Candida* problems or an intolerance to yeast as the dried fruit cannot be substituted.

115 g (4 oz/½ cup) dried apricots
5 ml (1 tsp) grated orange rind
55 g (2 oz/½ cup) nuts e.g. almonds, hazelnuts
6 puffed rice cakes or 55 g (2 oz/2 cups) puffed rice cereal
55 g (2 oz/½ cup) dried fruit e.g. raisins, apple, peach
115 ml (4 fl oz/½ cup) orange juice or water
55 g (2 oz/²⁄₃ cup) desiccated coconut
115 g (4 oz/1¹⁄₃ cups) ground almonds
extra desiccated coconut

1 Cut the apricots into small pieces and simmer in the orange juice and orange rind or water for approximately 5 minutes or until soft.
2 Chop the nuts into small pieces and toast in the oven or under the grill. Toast the desiccated coconut in the same way but make sure that it does not burn.
3 Break the puffed rice cakes into pieces and place in the food processor goblet. Add the coconut, the ground almonds, the apricot mixture and process until well mixed. You will need to stop the machine and scrape the mixture from the sides of the bowl once or twice as the mixture is quite sticky.
4 Turn the mixture out into a bowl and add the chopped toasted nuts and the chopped dried fruit. Mix by hand until the mixture forms a large ball.
5 Line a baking tray with foil or greaseproof paper and sprinkle with desiccated coconut. Spread the mixture out, levelling the surface, and sprinkle with more coconut. Press down well, cut into 12 or 16 pieces then leave to dry out, preferably overnight, before storing in an airtight container. Use within 1 week.

NUTTY CAROB SNACKS

55 g (2 oz/²/₃ cup) desiccated coconut   55 g (2 oz/¹/₂ cup) carob flour
115 g (4 oz/1 ¹/₃ cups) ground almonds 3 puffed rice cakes or 30 g
90 ml (6 tbsp) nut butter e.g.   (1 oz/1 cup) puffed rice cereal
   almond, cashew etc.   approximately 60 ml (4 tbsp) water

1 Place all the ingredients except the water into a food processor and mix well. Add sufficient water for the mixture to bind together when pressed.
2 Roll the mixture into walnut-sized balls and place on a tray. Leave to dry out overnight then store in an airtight container. Use within 1 week.

POPCORN

80 ml (3 rounded tbsp) popcorn

Method 1

Place the popcorn in a large bowl and cover with a large plate. Microwave on the highest setting for approximately 5 minutes until the popcorn has stopped popping.

Method 2

Heat 10 ml (1 dsp) of olive oil in a heavy-bottomed pan until hot. Add the corn, cover the pan with a lid and keep on a high heat until the corn has finished popping. Shake the pan regularly to prevent the corn sticking and burning.

CAROB BIRTHDAY CAKE

This cake contains rather too much oil to eat on a daily basis but enables you to celebrate special occasions without feeling the odd one out.

The above mixture can be made into 12 deep buns which will need cooking for approximately 20 minutes. The potato flour can be omitted and extra rice flour used if desired. An egg replacer does not substitute well in this recipe as it is difficult to make a light cake without eggs. If you do use one, add an extra 5 ml (1 tsp) potassium baking powder.

55 g (2 oz/¹/₃ cup) banana, sliced	2 eggs
55 g (2 oz/½ cup) carob flour	45 g (1½ oz/¼ cup) potato flour
70 g (2½ oz/½ cup) rice flour	20 ml (2 level dsp) potassium
115 ml (4 oz/½ cup) sunflower oil	baking powder
105 ml (7 tbsp/½ cup) soya milk or water	

1 In a food processor, mix all the ingredients until smooth. Alternatively, mash the banana well then add the beaten eggs and the remaining ingredients, beating well with a wooden spoon. Sieve the carob flour if it is lumpy.
2 Place in a greased, lined 18-cm (7-in) sandwich tin and bake in the middle of the oven at 330°F/170°C/gas mark 3 for 50–60 minutes. Do not undercook or the cake will tend to deflate on cooling.
3 Turn out onto a wire tray and cool.
4 When cool, cut the cake into 3 layers and sandwich together with carob cream made with 115 ml (4 fl oz/½ cup) of water instead of 140 ml (5 fl oz/²/₃ cup) (see Chapter 10, page 168). Top with carob cream and decorate with toasted nuts or desiccated coconut. Carob chocolate could be used to decorate the cake but check the ingredients first.

CHRISTMAS CAKE

This cake contains too much oil and dried fruit to be eaten often but is delicious for special occasions. Salt-free butter can be used to replace the oil.

170 g (6 oz/1 $^1/_6$ cups) dried dates
115 ml (4 fl oz/$^1/_2$ cup) sunflower oil
55 g (2 oz/$^1/_3$ cup) rice flour
455 g (1 lb/4 cups) mixed dried fruit e.g. raisins, currants, sultanas

140 ml (5 fl oz/$^2/_3$ cup) water
30 g (1 oz/$^1/_3$ cup) ground almonds
5 ml (1 tsp) mixed spice
3 eggs or egg replacer
55 g (2 oz/$^2/_3$ cup) soya flour
55 g (2 oz/$^1/_3$ cup) fine maize flour

1 Chop the dates into small pieces and place in a pan with the water. Bring to the boil and simmer over a low heat for approximately 10 minutes until the dates are soft. Cool.
2 Process or beat together the dates, oil, ground almonds, spices, eggs and flours until they are well blended.
3 Stir in the dried fruit and mix well by hand.
4 Place into a lined and greased 18-cm (6–8-in) cake tin and bake at 330°F/170°C/gas mark 3 for approximately 30 minutes, then lower the temperature to 290°F/145°C/gas mark 1 for a further 45 minutes.

ALMOND PASTE

55 g (2oz/$^1/_2$ cup) dried dates
60 ml (2 fl oz/$^1/_4$ cup) water
115 g (4 oz/1 $^1/_3$ cups) ground almonds
2 drops natural almond essence

1 Finely chop the dates and simmer in the water on a low heat until soft.
2 Process the dates, almonds and essence until the mixture starts to bind together. Press together any loose pieces and roll the mixture into a ball by hand.

3 Roll out the almond paste in rice flour to fit the Christmas Cake. Decorate with nuts if desired.

SIMNEL CAKE

Use half the almond paste, roll out into a circle and sandwich in the middle of the Christmas Cake mixture before cooking. Cook as above. When cool, use the remaining almond paste to decorate the top.

MINCEMEAT

225 g (8 oz/1¼ cups) dried apricots
565 g (1¼ lb/5 cups) cooking apples
3 ml (½ tsp) ground ginger
3 ml (½ tsp) nutmeg
3 ml (½ tsp) cinnamon

juice of 1 large orange
grated rind of 1 orange
340 ml (12 fl oz/1½ cups) water
455 g (1 lb/3 cups) mixed dried
    fruit e.g. raisins, currants,
    sultanas

1 Finely chop the dried apricots and grate the apples.
2 Put all the ingredients into a saucepan, bring to the boil and simmer gently for approximately 20 minutes, stirring occasionally to prevent sticking. Allow to cool.
3 Store in jars or Tupperware containers for no more than 3 weeks in the fridge and up to 6 months in the freezer.

MINCE PIES (12 PIES)

Pastry ingredients:

55 g (2 oz/^{2}/$_3$ cup) ground almonds	90 ml (6 tbsp) water
170 g (6 oz/1 cup) rice flour	60 ml (4 tbsp) sunflower oil
3 ml (½ tsp) cinnamon	60 ml (4 level tbsp) nut butter
2 ml (¼ tsp) ground cloves	(almond, cashew or hazelnut)

1 Place all the ingredients into the food processor and blend until well mixed. The mixture will still resemble breadcrumbs but will form into a pastry as you press it together by hand. If you do not have a food processor, mix the dry ingredients together, then the wet ingredients. Combine the two sets of ingredients with a fork, then press together by hand.

2 Divide the pastry in half and roll out each half sandwiched between clingfilm. This helps to prevent the pastry from breaking.

3 At this point you can either wrestle with the pastry to make small mince pies or give in to the fact that the pastry is quite brittle and make a large plate pie. You may still have to patch the pie but do not worry – it will taste fine.

4 Use the mincemeat to fill the pie or pies, cover with a pastry lid and press the pastry together at the edges.

5 Bake at 350°F/180°C/gas mark 4 for approximately 10–15 minutes for small pies and 20–25 minutes for the large pie until golden brown and crisp.

Desserts

I have tried to include a good selection of desserts so that treats are available for weekends, for entertaining or for those evenings when you just feel like something special. It has been necessary, however, to include dried fruits, tropical fruits and acidic fruits in quite a few recipes. As these desserts should not be eaten too regularly, try to eat starters rather than puddings on most days, and save desserts for the occasional meal.

Individuals with severe *Candida* problems or a yeast intolerance should avoid the recipes containing dried fruit.

APRICOT AND BANANA CHEESECAKE (SERVES 4)

Tofu may need to be avoided when initially treating *Candida albicans*.

Base

30 g (1 oz/$^1/_3$ cup) desiccated coconut	45 g (1$^1/_2$ oz/$^1/_3$ cup) hazelnuts
1 rice cake or 80 ml (4 tbsp) puffed rice cereal	hazelnuts to decorate

Topping

85 g (3 oz/$^1/_2$ cup) banana, chopped	55 g (2 oz/$^1/_4$ cup) dried apricots
290-g (10-oz) packet (1$^1/_4$ cups) firm silken tofu	2 ml ($^1/_4$ tsp) cinnamon
	2 ml ($^1/_4$ tsp) grated lemon rind

To make the base:
1 Toast the hazelnuts and coconut separately, either in the oven or under the grill, until golden brown. Allow to cool then rub the skins off the hazelnuts.
2 Place all the base ingredients into a food processor until the nuts are finely chopped and all the ingredients are mixed. Remove from the processor.

To make the topping:

1 Cut the apricots into small pieces and simmer in a small amount of water until soft. Sieve to remove the cooking liquid.
2 Process the apricots, banana, tofu, cinnamon and lemon rind until smooth.

To assemble:

1 Alternate two layers of both the base and topping ingredients (finishing with a layer of topping) either in a dish or, preferably, in four tall glasses or sundae dishes. Decorate with a few hazelnuts.

CAROB CREAM (SERVES 4)

Serve in sundae glasses decorated with toasted split almonds, or as a topping for other deserts.

115 g (4 oz/1 cup) cashew nuts
15 ml (1 tbsp) carob powder
toasted split almonds to decorate

140 ml (5 fl oz/^{2}/$_3$ cup) water or
soya or rice milk
2 large bananas

1 Place all the ingredients in a food processor for 2 minutes until smooth and creamy in texture.

CAROB CREAM DESSERT (SERVES 4)

Follow the recipe for Apricot and Banana Cheesecake *(see page 167)* but use the ingredients for Carob Cream *(see previous recipe)* instead of the apricot and banana topping. Assemble as directed.

APPLE CRUMBLE (SERVES 4)

Serve hot with Vanilla Custard *(see page 173)*, soya yogurt or Banana and Mango Ice Cream *(see page 177)*. If you prefer a sharper taste, substitute baking apples for two eating apples. Oat flakes could be used instead of the millet flakes if gluten is acceptable. Other fruit can be substituted for the apples, such as plums or cherries, but the fruit needs to be naturally sweet as no sugar is added.

4 eating apples	30 ml (2 tbsp) water
85 g (3 oz/1 cup) millet flakes	30 g (1 oz/$^1/_6$ cup) brown rice flour
55 g (2 oz/$^2/_3$cup) ground almonds	30 g (1 oz/$^1/_3$cup) desiccated
3 ml ($^1/_2$ tsp) cinnamon	coconut
20 ml (2 dsp) sunflower oil	30 ml (2 tbsp) sunflower seeds

1 Peel and core the apples and finely slice into an ovenproof dish. Pour the water over the apples.
2 To make the crumble, place the millet flakes, rice flour, ground almonds, coconut and cinnamon into a bowl and rub in the oil by hand. Spread the crumble over the fruit and sprinkle the sunflower seeds on top.
3 Bake for 20 minutes at 400°F/200°C/gas mark 6 until the topping is brown and the apples are tender.

APPLE PIE (SERVES 4)

The pastry in this pie is really crisp and delicious but difficult to handle. I find it easier to make saucer pies rather than one big pie. Use baking apples if you prefer a sharper taste or a mixture of the two. Serve with Vanilla Custard (see page 173), soya yogurt or Banana and Mango Ice Cream (see page 177). Try pies made from other sweet fruits, such as plums, cherries and blackberries.

1 portion pastry (see recipe for Mince	4 eating apples
Pies, Chapter 9, page 166)	3 ml ($^1/_2$ tsp) cinnamon
2 ml ($^1/_4$ tsp) ground cloves	

1 Follow the instuctions for making pastry from the Mince Pie recipe and use half the pastry to line a pie dish.
2 Peel and core the apples and finely slice into the pie. Sprinkle the apples with the spices. Cover the pie with the remaining pastry, wetting the edges to seal the pie.

3 Bake at 350°F/180°C/gas mark 4 for approximately 20–25 minutes or until the pastry is golden brown and crisp and the filling cooked.

BAKED APPLES (SERVES 4)

Serve hot with Vanilla Custard *(see page 173)*, soya yogurt or just as they are. The apples could be stuffed with dried fruit before baking, if this is tolerated.

90 ml (3 fl oz/^{1}/$_3$ cup) orange juice, apple juice or water	4 eating apples
	grated rind of ^{1}/$_2$ orange
3 ml (^{1}/$_2$ tsp) grated ginger	3 ml (^{1}/$_2$ tsp) mixed spice

1 Wash and core the apples. Place in a casserole dish that is not too large so that the apples are supported by the sides. Prick the skins with a knife to prevent them bursting.
2 Mix the fruit juice or water with the orange rind, the ginger and the mixed spice, and pour around the apples in the casserole dish.
3 Cover the apples and bake in the centre of the oven at 400°F/ 200°C/gas mark 6 for approximately 30 minutes until the apples are just soft but not mushy.

RICE PUDDING (SERVES 4)

15 ml (1 tbsp) chopped dates (optional)	90 ml (3 fl oz/^{1}/$_3$ cup) water
570 ml (1 pint/2^1/$_2$ cups) soya, rice or almond milk	115 g (4 oz/1 cup) brown rice flakes
3 ml (^{1}/$_2$ tsp) ground cinnamon	30 g (1 oz/^{1}/$_4$ cup) sultanas (optional)
4 drops natural vanilla extract or 1 vanilla pod	grated nutmeg

1 Place the chopped dates in the water and simmer until they are soft and mushy. Mix in the milk a little at a time, beating the dates well so that they disintegrate, sweetening the milk.

2 Place the milk, rice flakes, cinnamon, sultanas and vanilla into a greased casserole dish. Sprinkle the surface liberally with grated nutmeg.
3 Bake at 400°F/200°C/gas mark 6 for approximately 1 hour, stirring occasionally.

ALMOND FRUIT BAKE (SERVES 4)

Ground rice is not the same as rice flour. It is more coarsely ground. In winter, when a good selection of fresh fruit is not available, try serving with a mixture of fresh and stewed fruit, such as prune and pear or apricot and apple.

30 g (1 oz/^{1}/$_6$ cup) ground rice
680 g (1½ lb/3–4 cups) mixed fresh
   sweet fruit e.g. cherries, apples,
   pears, peaches, apricots, plums

85 g (3 oz/1 cup) ground almonds
570 ml (1 pint/2½ cups) soya,
   rice or almond milk
3 ml (½ tsp) natural vanilla
   extract

1 Mix the ground rice with 60 ml (2 fl oz/¼ cup) of cold milk. Bring the remaining milk to the boil, then add the ground rice mixture, stirring all the time until it returns to the boil. Simmer, stirring constantly, for 2 minutes.
2 Add the ground almonds and vanilla extract and stir well.
3 Pour into a shallow greased gratin dish.
4 Remove the stones or cores from the fruit where necessary and slice the larger fruits. Arrange the fruit on top of the ground rice mixture in an attractive pattern, placing the cut sides downwards. Press the fruit down well.
5 Bake for approximately 30 minutes, or until the fruit is cooked, at 400°F/200°C/gas mark 6. Serve hot or cold.

STUFFED PEACHES (4)

Almond Paste (see Chapter 9, page 164)   4 large peaches
30 ml (2 tbsp) toasted slivered almonds

1 Make the Almond Paste as directed.
2 Halve and stone the peaches and place in a baking dish, cut side uppermost (cut a little slice off the rounded edge, if necessary, to help them remain stable).
3 Divide the Almond Paste into 8 pieces, roll into balls and place a ball in the centre of each peach half.
4 Bake, covered, for 10 minutes, then uncovered for a further 10 minutes at 400°F/200°C/gas mark 6. The peaches should be soft and the filling just starting to brown.
5 Sprinkle with toasted slivered almonds before serving either hot or cold.

FRIED BANANAS (SERVES 4)

Serve with Vanilla Custard *(see page 173)*, Banana and Mango Ice Cream *(see page 177)*, soya yogurt or just as they are. If you are allowed dairy produce, using low-salt butter to fry the bananas will give added flavour.

4 bananas
5 ml (1 tsp) sunflower oil
3 ml (½ tsp) grated lemon rind
3 ml (½ tsp) grated orange rind
3 ml (½ tsp) cinnamon
juice of 1 orange
15 ml (1 tbsp) toasted slivered almonds

1 Peel the bananas and fry quickly in the oil until beginning to brown and soften on the outside. This will take only 2–3 minutes.
2 Add the remaining ingredients, mix well and serve immediately.

VANILLA CUSTARD (SERVES 4)

If you cannot tolerate eggs, use 60 ml (4 level tbsp) maize meal instead of the 30 ml (2 tbsp) in the list of ingredients. A vanilla pod could be used instead of the vanilla extract. The dates can be omitted if dried fruit is not acceptable.

30 ml (2 tbsp) finely chopped dates (optional)	60 ml (2 fl oz/¼ cup) water
570 ml (1 pint/2½ cups) soya, rice or almond milk	30 ml (2 tbsp) fine maize meal
	2 eggs, beaten
	3 ml (½ tsp) natural vanilla extract

1 Place the dates in the water in a saucepan and simmer until they are soft. Mix the maize meal and the milk and add to the dates a little at a time, beating well to enable the dates to disintegrate and sweeten the milk.
2 Add the eggs and vanilla extract.
3 Gradually bring the mixture to the boil, stirring constantly. Lower the heat and simmer for 1 minute. Do not boil rapidly or the eggs will curdle.

SPONGE AND CUSTARD

Serve the Vanilla Custard with warm Carrot and Coconut Cake *(see Chapter 9, page 157)*, Apple, Date and Nut Muffins *(see Chapter 9, page 155)* or Ginger and Orange Cake *(see Chapter 9, page 156)*.

PRUNES AND CUSTARD

Serve the Vanilla Custard with stewed prunes.

BANANA CUSTARD

Cut 4 bananas into slices and add to the Vanilla Custard when it has cooled a little. Serve warm or allow to cool before serving.

BLACK FOREST TRIFLE

Crumble $^1/_3$ of a carob birthday cake into a serving dish. Mix in two small tins of fruit in natural juice ie. strawberries, raspberries, blackberries. Pour over vanilla custard, allow to cool and serve.

BAKED EGG CUSTARD (SERVES 4)

The custard will continue cooking for a little while once out of the oven, so remove while still a little soft. Serve with stewed dried fruit, Fried Bananas *(see page 172)* or Fresh Fruit Salad *(see page 175)*. A vanilla pod could be used instead of the extract but will need soaking in the warm milk for 30 minutes to allow the flavour to be absorbed. Remove the pod before baking.

3 eggs, beaten
nutmeg
570 ml (1 pint/2½ cups) soya,
  rice or almond milk

3 ml (½ tsp) natural vanilla
  extract

1 Grease an ovenproof dish and put in the beaten eggs.
2 Warm the milk in a saucepan, then pour over the eggs, stirring thoroughly.
3 Mix in the vanilla extract and sprinkle the surface with nutmeg.
4 Place the dish in a baking tray containing cold water. Then place the two dishes in the oven.
5 Bake at 325°F/170°C/gas mark 3 for approximately 30 minutes or until the mixture is just setting in the centre. Do not over-cook or the mixture will boil and curdle.

FRUIT FOOL (SERVES 4)

Serve in sundae glasses either just as it is or decorated with chopped nuts.

455 g (1 lb/4 cups) fresh or frozen sweet fruit e.g. apricots, peaches, cherries, strawberries, plums, apples

115 g (4 oz/1 cup) cashew nuts
140 ml (5 fl oz/$^2/_3$ cup) soya, rice or almond milk

1 Place the cashew nuts in a food processor until finely ground.
2 Add the milk and process again until a smooth cream is obtained.
3 If using soft fresh fruit, such as peaches or strawberries, add these to the cashew cream and process again. If using harder fresh fruit, such as apples or plums, stew the fruit in a little water until soft and then add to the cashew cream, reserving the cooking liquid unless needed to make the mixture soft. If using frozen fruit, defrost and add to the cashew cream, again reserving any juices unless needed.

FRUIT FOOL ICE CREAM (SERVES 4)

Follow the previous recipe but use frozen fruit. Do not defrost but add to the cashew nut cream through the processor funnel while the machine is on high power. Process until smooth and serve immediately or return to the freezer.

FRESH FRUIT SALAD (SERVES 4)

To liven up a fresh fruit salad in winter, use a little frozen fruit, such as raspberries and blackberries, or an occasional tin of fruit in natural juice as a base.

You do not have to use all the fruits available for a fruit salad. Try just serving 2–3 fruits, such as:

- melon and strawberry
- pear, sharron fruit and raspberries
- melon, kiwi fruit and blackberry
- orange and date
- melon and black grape

A delicious dessert can be made for entertaining by making a fruit salad of tropical fruits, such as sharron fruit, dates, bananas, and mango, and mixing with 425 ml (¾ pint/2 cups) of yogurt (preferably Greek) instead of the fruit juice. Add ½ cup of toasted flaked almonds and assemble just before serving to prevent the yogurt becoming watery and the nuts soft.

285 ml (10 fl oz/1 ⅓ cups) fresh fruit juice e.g. apple, orange, pineapple
680 g (1½ lb/3–4 cups) fresh fruit selected from the following:

- apple
- fresh dates
- orange
- pear
- pineapple
- peach
- plums
- sharron fruit
- strawberries

- banana
- grapes
- blackberries
- melon
- mango
- passion fruit
- cherries
- raspberries

1 Pour the fruit juice into a serving dish.
2 Peel, core and prepare the fruit and cut into even-sized pieces.
3 Add to the fruit juice, mix well and chill before serving.

FRUIT TERRINE (SERVES 4)

Gelozone is the vegetarian equivalent of gelatine. Use juice from a carton rather then freshly squeezed as this is slightly less acidic. Other fruits can be substituted, such as pear, peach, sharron fruit, bananas and strawberries.

115 g (4 oz/⅔ cup) cherries
1 mango
285 ml (10 fl oz/1 ⅓ cups) fruit juice

115 g (4 oz/⅔ cup) grapes
¼ melon
5 ml (1 tsp) Gelozone

1 Peel and stone the fruit and dice the mango and melon. Layer the fruit in a terrine or loaf tin.

2 Mix the Gelozone with the fruit juice in a pan and stir until dissolved.
3 Bring just to the boil then pour over the fruit in the terrine while still hot.
4 Refrigerate until set, then serve cut into slices.

FRUIT PLATTER

The same ingredients can be used as for the previous recipe but served on individual plates (preferably white). Pour the fruit juice and Gelozone onto plates and arrange the fruit in an attractive pattern in the middle. Allow to set as before.

JELLY

A plain jelly can be made for children by using 570 ml (1 pint/2½ cups) of fruit juice and 10 ml (1 level dsp) Gelozone. Dissolve the Gelozone in the fruit juice in a pan then bring to the boil, stirring all the time. Place in a serving dish or mould and allow to cool in the fridge. Serve with fresh fruit, ice cream, yogurt or custard.

BANANA AND MANGO ICE CREAM

Serve the ice cream just as it is or with other puddings. Vary by adding toasted nuts, desiccated coconut or 15 ml (1 tbsp) carob flour. Finely chopped crystallized ginger or candied peel can be added for those allowed a little sugar, or for a dessert when entertaining.

140 ml (5 fl oz/²/₃ cup) soya, rice or almond milk

1 large mango
3 bananas

1 Peel and slice the bananas and freeze in a container so that the bananas are not squashed together but will separate when frozen.
2 Peel and stone the mango and dice the flesh. Freeze in the same way as the bananas.

3 Pour the milk into a food processor and switch on at full power. I wrap a tea towel round the processor to stop the milk splashing. Gradually add the banana and mango pieces through the funnel, stopping if necessary to break the fruit up if it starts to stick together. Eventually you will obtain a smooth, creamy ice cream.

4 Serve at once or return to the freezer. If left in the freezer for long, the ice cream will set quite hard and will then need to be left out to stand for approximately 20 minutes before serving.

BANANA AND PEACH ICE CREAM

Substitute 2 peaches for the mango in the previous recipe.

STRAWBERRY AND BANANA ICE CREAM

Substitute 285 ml (10 oz/2 cups) strawberries for the mango in the recipe for Banana and Mango Ice Cream *(see page 177)*. Allow the strawberries to thaw for approximately 5 minutes before processing as they are very solid when frozen.

STRAWBERRY AND PEACH SORBET

Freeze 285 ml (10 oz/2 cups) strawberries and 2 peaches. Thaw for approximately 5 minutes then process along with 115 ml (4 fl oz/½ cup) fruit juice (orange, apple etc.) or water.

A wide range of ice creams and sorbets can be made using the above methods and substituting different fruits. Yogurt can be used instead of the milk for another variation.

SWEET SOUFFLÉ OMELETTE (SERVES 2)

Mincemeat *(see Chapter 9, page 165)* or Marmalade *(see Chapter 1, page 52)* could be used instead of the stewed fruit.

2 eggs	30 ml (2 tbsp) water
5 ml (1 tsp) sunflower oil	90 ml (6 tbsp) stewed fresh fruit e.g. apples, plums, apricots

1 Separate the egg yolks from the whites, putting them in two bowls. Add the water to the yolks and mix well.
2 Whisk the egg whites until stiff and fold gently into the egg yolks with a metal spoon.
3 Cook in the sunflower oil in an omelette pan over a medium heat until the underside of the omelette is golden brown.
4 Place the pan under the grill until the omelette is brown on top and set.
5 Spread the stewed fruit over the omelette and fold in half. Serve at once.

STUFFED PANCAKES (SERVES 4)

1 egg	115 g (4 oz/^{2}/$_3$ cup) rice flour
3 ml (½ tsp) cinnamon	2 ml (¼ tsp) lemon rind
170 ml (6 fl oz/¾ cup) soya or rice milk	60 ml (2 fl oz/¼ cup) water
5 ml (1 tsp) potassium baking powder	10 ml (1 dsp) sunflower oil

1 Blend all the ingredients except the oil in the food processor. If mixing by hand, beat the eggs then add the remaining ingredients except the oil and beat well.
2 Oil a pan or griddle and cook 4 pancakes. Turn the pancakes as soon as they are puffed and full of bubbles.

BANANA PANCAKES

Roll each pancake round a small peeled banana. Heat through and serve with soya yogurt, Banana and Mango Ice Cream *(see page 177)*, Carob Cream *(see page 168)* or Vanilla Custard *(see page 173)*.

SUMMER FRUIT PANCAKES

Gently stew a selection of summer fruits, such as strawberries, raspberries, redcurrants and blackberries. The juice could be thickened with a little arrowroot or Gelozone if desired. Serve layered with the pancakes.

ORANGE PANCAKES

Fold the pancakes into quarters and warm in the pan with 140 ml (¼ pint/⅔ cup) orange juice, the grated rind of ½ an orange and a few orange segments.

APPLE PANCAKES

Serve the pancakes with stewed apple sprinkled with nutmeg and cinnamon. Accompany with Vanilla Custard *(see page 173)* or Mango and Banana Ice Cream *(see page 177)* if desired.

MELON WITH MANGO SAUCE (SERVES 4)

1 small or ½ large melon	1 large or 2 small mangos
3 passion fruit	

1 Cube or ball the melon flesh. Peel the mango and slice the flesh from the stone.
2 Liquidize the mango, the flesh from the passion fruit and a quarter of the melon to make a smooth sauce. If you have used a melon baller for the melon, liquidize the leftover pieces of melon.
3 Sieve the sauce to remove the passion fruit seeds. Serve the melon in sundae glasses with the sauce poured over.

SPICED PEARS (SERVES 4)

Serve hot or cold just as they are or with vanilla custard, soya yogurt or Banana and Mango Ice Cream *(see page 177)*.

3 large firm pears
3 ml (½ tsp) cinnamon
115 ml (4 fl oz/½ cup) apple juice

3 ml (½ tsp) ground cardamom
2 ml (¼ tsp) ground cloves

1 Peel and quarter the pears and cut away the cores.
2 Cut the pears into 2-cm (½-in) lengthwise slices and place in an ovenproof dish.
3 Sprinkle with the spices and pour the apple juice over.
4 Cover and bake at 400°F/200°C/gas mark 6 for approximately 20 minutes or until tender.

POACHED PEARS WITH CAROB CUSTARD (SERVES 4)

Serve hot or cold.

2 large pears
45 ml (3 tbsp) water
80 ml (4 rounded tbsp) rice flour
30 ml (2 level tbsp) carob flour
710 ml (1¼ pints/3 ⅙ cups) soya, rice or almond milk

30 ml (2 tbsp) desiccated coconut to decorate

1 Peel, core and quarter the pears and simmer gently in the water until just cooked.
2 Mix the rice flour and the carob flour with a little cold milk in a pan until smooth. Add the remaining milk and bring to the boil, stirring all the time. Simmer for 1 minute.
3 Serve the pears with the carob custard and sprinkled with the coconut.

CHRISTMAS PUDDING

Makes 3 puddings to serve 4 people. I freeze any puddings which will not be used within one week as they will not keep for too long. Serve with vanilla custard.

1 portion of Christmas Cake recipe (see page 164)
20 ml (2 level dsp) potassium baking powder

2 large grated carrots
225 g (8 oz/2 cups) baking apples, peeled and grated

1 Mix the Christmas Cake ingredients as per the recipe on page 164. (To save time, I double the quantity and make both puddings and cake on the same day.)
2 Mix in the grated carrots, apples and baking powder.
3 Divide the mixture into greased pudding basins, depending on the size of the puddings you require.
4 Steam, pressure cook or microwave the puddings according to their size. The 4-person pudding will take 30 minutes in the pressure cooker, 2 hours over boiling water and 12 minutes in the microwave on power level 5.

Useful Addresses

SPNT (Society for the Promotion of Nutritional Therapy)
PO Box 47, Heathfield, East Sussex TN21 8ZX. Tel. 01435 867007
An educational and campaigning organization with lay and practitioner members. Send SAE and £1 for information and a list of your nearest qualified nutritional therapists.

ION (The Institute of Optimum Nutrition)
Blades Court, Deodar Road, London SW15 2NU. Tel. 0181 877 9993
ION exists as an independent charity to help you achieve optimum health. ION offers short courses, home-study courses, books, a magazine, consultations and a Nutrition Consultants diploma course.

Cytoplan Ltd
Hanley Workshop, Hanley Swan, Worcs. WR8 0DX. Tel. 01684 310099
Stockists of food state supplements plus nutritional advice line.

Higher Nature Ltd.
Burwash Common, East Sussex TN19 7LX. Tel. 01435 882880
Catalogue of nutritional supplements and free magazine available on request. Also a nutrition helpline for your queries or nutrition consultations by phone or in person.

York Nutritional Laboratory
Tudor House, Lysander Close, Clifton Moor, York YO3 4XB.
Tel. 01904 690640
Offers cytotoxic blood tests for allergies and intolerances.

Allergy Care (Foodwatch)
Pollards Yard, Wood Street, Taunton, Somerset TA1 1UP.
Tel. 01823 325023
Mail-order suppliers of alternative and substitute food products. Also a team of qualified allergy testers (using vega testing) working in over 500 centres throughout the UK.

Charles Gordon
Gordon House, Little Mead Industrial Estate, Cranleigh,
Surrey GU6 8ND. Tel. 01483 267707
Suppliers of mustard flour with no other added ingredients and English mustard with salt, water and spices added.

Index